D0844107

The Great Declaration

The Great

*A Book
for
Young Americans*

Declaration

WRITTEN AND EDITED

by

Henry Steele Commager

DRAWINGS BY DONALD BOLOGNESE

THE BOBBS-MERRILL COMPANY INC.

Publishers

INDIANAPOLIS • NEW YORK

COPYRIGHT © 1958 BY THE BOBBS-MERRILL COMPANY, INC.
PRINTED IN THE UNITED STATES OF AMERICA
LIBRARY OF CONGRESS CATALOG CARD NUMBER: 58-12915
Eleventh Printing

ACKNOWLEDGMENTS

Text and Picture Sources

Text

The following, which have been of special value in the writing of this story, are gratefully acknowledged:

The Autobiography of Benjamin Rush, edited by George W. Corner (Princeton University Press for the American Philosophical Society, 1948).

Benjamin Franklin, by Carl Van Doren (New York: Viking Press, 1938).

Papers of Thomas Jefferson, edited by Julian P. Boyd (Princeton University Press, 1950-1955).

Warren-Adams Letters (Boston: Massachusetts Historical Society, 1917-1925).

William and Mary Quarterly, Volume XVI (College of William and Mary, Institute of Early American Culture, Williamsburg, Virginia, 1908).

Pictures

Page

10 Thomas Jefferson. Portrait by Thomas Sully. Courtesy Library of Congress.

15 The retreat from Concord. Engraving by James Smillie from a painting by Chappel.

(Continued on p. 108)

9 73.3
C.1

THE LIBRARY
CHILDREN'S LITERATURE COLLECTION
HUMBOLDT STATE UNIVERSITY
ARCATA, CALIFORNIA 95521

To
ROBBIE
with love

CONTENTS

LIST OF ILLUSTRATIONS

The Great Declaration

Thomas Jefferson

I "WHEN IN THE COURSE OF HUMAN EVENTS"

"When in the Course of human events . . . We hold these truths to be self-evident. . . ." What grand words these are! They bring before us the whole sweep of history; they tie history to morality and truth. And this is as it should be, because the Declaration of Independence is both a great historical and a great moral document. It is not too much to say that it is the most important document in modern history. It ushered onto the stage of history a new nation—the United States of America. It opened up an era of revolutions—revolutions of colonies against mother countries, and of North America, South America, Asia and Africa against Europe. It set forth, in words of matchless force and beauty, a body of political principles which spread throughout the globe and came to be accepted almost everywhere as just and wise.

All these things affected the whole world eventually; they affected America immediately. The Declaration of Independence was *our* birth certificate; it announced *our* independence, inspired *our* revolution, provided *our* political principles. It is universal, but it is primarily American, and it is natural that we should be interested in every detail of its history.

How did it come about, and why? Who wrote it? What did it say? How was it adopted, and how received? Why has it survived and flourished through the years?

When we ask how the Declaration of Independence came about, and why it was necessary, we are asking big questions. We are indeed asking for a history of the causes of the American Revolution. That is a large order, larger than we can fill here and now. We will have to content ourselves with giving something of the background of the Revolution and then get on to the Declaration itself.

What was the Revolution about? Well, it was about a lot of things, but mostly about home rule. For over a century the American colonies had been part of the British Empire, but during most of that period they had pretty well managed their own affairs. Now, by the 1770's, they had "come of age." They occupied an immense territory, stretching all the way from Maine to Georgia—a territory much larger than Britain. They were two and a half million strong—and that at a time when the population of the mother country was only eight million or so—and they were growing all the time, growing faster than any other people on the earth. They were intelligent, industrious and prosperous, and, most important, they were free. They had long been accustomed to governing themselves, and they had no intention of giving up their self-government. They were like a young man coming of age, suspicious of every attempt by his parents to run his life for him, eager to strike out for himself, strong and self-confident.

And this was just the time the mother country chose to tighten its controls—to allow her American colonials not more freedom but less. Nothing could have been more shortsighted. And not only did Britain try to tighten the reins of Empire; she made it clear, too, that she regarded the American colonials as inferiors, whose business it was to fit their interest and convenience to the interest and convenience of the mother country. Indeed in one famous act the British Parliament said just exactly that. "The American colonies are"—so read the act—"subordinate unto the Parliament of Great Britain *in all cases whatsoever.*" Can you imagine anything sillier than that—as if any people are ever subordinate *in all cases whatsoever!*

Trouble had been brewing ever since 1763, when the British, having finally acquired all of French Canada, took over Florida as well, and started to organize this great North American empire into a neat and

12

symmetrical package. Parliament passed a whole series of laws, all directed to the same end: to make the colonials pay their own way, and to fit them into the larger British political and economic scheme.

It was an attempt to use the Americans to help one particular British business interest that brought matters to a head. Parliament had put a tax on all the tea imported into the American colonies. The Americans liked their tea, but thought the tax illegal. Then, to make matters worse, Parliament came to the rescue of the great East India Company by giving it a monopoly—exclusive control—on the importation of tea to the colonies. Nobody likes taxes, and nobody likes a monopoly, and when these are imposed from the outside, and for the benefit of outsiders, they seem particularly outrageous.

The Boston Tea Party

This was not, perhaps, the best issue on which to revolt, this matter of the tea. But to start with, Americans didn't plan to revolt; they just wanted to protest. And protest they did. Late in the afternoon of December 16, 1773, a band of Bostonians, dressed like Mohawk

13

and Narragansett Indians (pretty cold, that), stormed down to the wharves, boarded three ships and threw overboard into the dancing waves 342 chests of tea. That was the Boston Tea Party.

That lawless act—for no matter how justified it may seem, there is no doubt that it was lawless—set off a chain reaction which eventually exploded into revolution and independence.

To punish Boston and the Massachusetts Bay Colony, Parliament passed a series of acts known as the Intolerable Acts: the name speaks for itself. The effect of these was to set up a military government under the British in Massachusetts, and to shut Boston off from the rest of America by closing the port and forbidding all trade. The purpose, of course, was to make the Bostonians feel guilty, and to force them not only to pay for the tea they had destroyed, but to give up still more of their self-government. The result (as so often) was just the opposite. A British general—Thomas Gage—now sat in the governor's mansion, and red-coated soldiers swarmed the streets of the ancient town, but they did not overawe the Bostonians. The Massachusetts patriots simply set up a government of their own, and it was this government that the people obeyed. As for isolating Boston, that too proved a failure. Overnight Boston became a martyr, and everywhere the American people made its cause their own. Each colony in America rallied to Boston's support, and soon, from almost every town and county, came herds of cattle, flocks of sheep, wagonloads of grain, money and supplies, to enable the Bostonians to hold out.

Nor was this all. The new "tough" policy of Parliament forced the colonies to unite in opposition, from New Hampshire to Georgia. In the fall of 1774, representatives from twelve American colonies met in Philadelphia to form the First Continental Congress—the beginning of American union. Led by men like Samuel and John Adams, Patrick Henry and Richard Henry Lee, the First Congress decided on resistance to British oppression.

Then came the battles of Lexington and Concord. The British commander, General Gage, decided to seize powder and military supplies that had been collected in the village of Concord, about thirty miles

14

The Redcoats Retreat from Concord

outside Boston, and—for good measure—to seize those two trouble-makers, Sam Adams and John Hancock, at the same time. Early on the morning of April 19 a column of redcoats marched out along the country road to Concord. Paul Revere and William Dawes—those two horsemen of the Revolution—had already spread the word, world at that time, but eventually, for the reverberations of that shot are still echoing.

With that the war was on. Twenty thousand patriots besieged the British in Boston. When the Americans tried to take the offensive, however, and seize Bunker's Hill, the British attacked them by land and by sea and drove them off—but at a cruel cost. This victory, if it can be called a victory, did the British no good. The siege was renewed; the lines were drawn ever tighter; and in the end they were forced to give up and sail away. Meantime the war, at first confined to Massachusetts, had spread; up in New York the fort of Ticonderoga fell to two patriot leaders, Benedict Arnold and Ethan Allen. Down in Virginia the royal governor was driven from his palace, and eventually from the colony. There was fighting in the Carolinas, too—fighting which showed that Americans everywhere meant business.

Just what business did they mean, anyway? Did they mean war? Did they mean independence?

Writing many years later, the onetime royal governor of Massachusetts, Thomas Hutchinson, alleged that the Americans had been working secretly for independence ever since the days of the quarrel over the Stamp Act, back in 1765. And in his old age John Adams, who probably knew as much about the Revolution as any man in America, gave support to this charge. The Revolution, he told an old friend, "was in the minds of the people, and in the union of the colonies, both of which were accomplished before hostilities commenced."

Yet at almost the same time, Adams was writing that though the colonies had long wanted to be independent of the King, "for my part there was not a moment during the Revolution when I would not have given everything I ever possessed for a restoration of the state of things before the contest began."

Of course Governor Hutchinson's suspicions of intrigue were nonsense. And once they had voted independence, neither Adams nor his friends wanted to go back to being colonies—even self-governing

16

colonies. But up to the time of the Declaration of Independence it was touch and go. Even after the battles of Lexington and Concord and Bunker's Hill there were zealous American patriots who still thought and talked in terms of reconciliation—John Jay in New

The Attack on Bunker's Hill

York, John Dickinson in Pennsylvania—yes, even Washington and Jefferson in Virginia.

Most Americans, then, were reluctant to plunge into independence or to challenge the might of Britain. Far from being radical (that is, rash, headstrong and violent) they were moderate (that is, prudent and cautious). There were, of course, exceptions—men like the fiery

17

Sam Adams or the reckless Tom Paine, or the uncompromising Patrick Henry, ready to break with England at whatever cost. But the great majority of those who in the end voted for independence were not, at the beginning, rebels. It was the war that made them rebels.

Yet by July 1776 the Second Continental Congress voted unanimously for independence. What brought about the change?

Three things. First, it became clear that George III had no intention of meeting the American demands, or of making any important concessions to those he regarded as wicked "rebels." Second, it became clear that if Americans were united, and could count on some help from France, they had a very good chance to win a war; nobody had quite believed that before Bunker's Hill. And third was the influence of a remarkable pamphlet called *Common Sense*. Written by Tom Paine, newly arrived in America, this pamphlet argued that it was ridiculous for a continent to belong to a little island, and that independence was merely the common sense of the matter. Paine's simple but powerful arguments appealed equally to the man at the plow and in the street, the soldier in the camp and the statesman at his desk in the Continental Congress. It ran through the colonies like a prairie fire. It made converts everywhere.

Thus by early spring of 1776 the movement for independence was gathering force and speed. The Congress in Philadelphia showed more boldness: in rapid succession it organized a Navy, it armed privateers—privately owned merchant vessels—stopped trade with the mother country, opened American ports to the trade of all the rest fell in line. Now, indeed, as John Adams wrote, "every day rolls in upon us Independence like a torrent." May 15 was in many ways the decisive day: on that day Virginia, oldest, most populous and most powerful of the states, voted for independence, and on that day, too, Congress formally told the states to form their own independent governments.

Now it was only a question of time. New England and the South had both swung over to independence; only the Middle States held back. There the moderates were still in control—men like John Dickinson and James Wilson in Pennsylvania, who were good patriots, but timid and fearful of all the changes that a revolution might bring. When on June 7 Richard Henry Lee of Virginia introduced a resolution for independence, the moderates were strong enough to postpone a vote for three weeks, during which they tried to rally support for a prudent course in their states. But prudence is never very popular; and certainly it was not in midsummer of 1776. When on July 1 Dickinson tried to stem the tide for independence, he was instead caught up in it and swept away. And on July 2 independence was voted without a dissenting voice.

Meantime Congress had appointed a committee of five to prepare a declaration that would explain and justify the vote for independence. With great good sense this committee assigned the job to its youngest member, Thomas Jefferson of Virginia. Jefferson's declaration, somewhat changed by the committee, was submitted to Congress on June 28, debated on the second, third and fourth of July, and passed on that now famous day. As for those signatures that stand out so boldly on the bottom of the page, most of them were added, in a rather casual fashion, almost a month later.

No one, not even Jefferson, played a larger role in making thirteen colonies into a single nation than stanch John Adams, and no one rejoiced more deeply when this "greatest question which ever was debated in America" was decided the right way. And it was Adams who, a few hours after the fateful vote, wrote to his wife Abigail these moving lines:

19

I am well aware of the toil and blood and treasure it will cost us to maintain this declaration and support and defend these states. Yet through all the gloom I can see the rays of ravishing light and glory. I can see that the end is more than worth all the means, and that posterity will triumph in that day's transaction.[1]

Let us turn, now, to the details—details that will never lose their fascination. We begin by introducing some of the leading actors in the great historical drama.

II THE FOUNDING FATHERS

The First Continental Congress, which had organized resistance to the mother country, had come to a close October 26, 1774. Before its members went home, they arranged for the meeting of their successor. The Second Continental Congress, which met in the State House in Philadelphia on May 10, 1775, is probably the most famous and certainly the most important Congress in our history. For it not only declared independence, but won it as well, and what is more, it laid the foundations for the American union. We ought to get acquainted with its members; fortunately one of them, Dr. Benjamin Rush, has given us a set of pen portraits of them.

First let us get acquainted with the artist himself. Benjamin Rush was only thirty when the war broke out. But, as with so many other young men of his day (for it was a young men's war), he had already achieved fame. At the age of twenty-one he sailed for Edinburgh, then the mecca of all the medical students of the English-speaking world. While there he studied not only medicine, but also philosophy, for Edinburgh had the liveliest intellectual society of any city in Britain at the time as well as the best medical school. On a visit to London, Rush came under the influence of his fellow townsman, Dr. Benjamin Franklin, who helped advance his bold thinking about government.

Back in Philadelphia young Dr. Rush rose rapidly to eminence. Within a few years he was a leading physician, professor at the new College of Philadelphia, member of the already famous American Philosophical Society, a zealous reformer and an ardent patriot. One of the first to champion independence, Rush was elected to the Continental Congress and thus had the good fortune to be one of the "signers." Among other things Rush early recognized the genius of Tom Paine, and encouraged him to write *Common Sense*, of which we shall hear more. In 1777 Rush became surgeon general of the Armies of the Middle Department, in which job he managed to make as many enemies as friends. It may be said of Dr. Rush that he knew everybody and took everybody's measure—sometimes most unfairly. Certainly he knew all the Founding Fathers, and the following portraits, painted a short time after the Revolution, were all made from personal acquaintance.

John Hancock, of Massachusetts. He was a man of plain understanding, and good education. He was fond of the ceremonies of public life, but wanted industry and punctuality in business. His conversation was desultory, and his manners much influenced by frequent attacks of the gout, which gave a hypochondriacal peevishness to his temper. With all these infirmities he was a disinterested patriot, and made large sacrifices of an ample estate to the liberties and independence of his country.

John Hancock

Samuel Adams

Samuel Adams, of Massachusetts. He was near sixty years of age when he took his seat in Congress, but possessed all the vigor of mind of a young man of five and twenty. He was a republican in principle and manners. He once acknowledged to me "that the independence of the United States upon Great Britain had been the first wish of his heart seven years before the war." About the same time he said to me "if it were revealed to him that 999 Americans out of 1000 would perish in a war for liberty, he would vote for that war, rather than see his country enslaved. The sur-

23

vivors in such a war, though few (he said), would propagate a
nation of freemen." He abhorred a standing army, and used to
say that they were the "shoeblacks of society." . . . He loved
simplicity and economy in the administration of government, and
despised the appeals which are made to the eyes and ears of the
common people in order to govern them.

He considered national happiness and the public patronage of
religion as inseparably connected; and so great was his regard for
public worship, as the means of promoting religion, that he con-
stantly attended divine service in the German church in York
town while the Congress sat there, when there was no service in
their chapel, although he was ignorant of the German language.
His morals were irreproachable, and even ambition and avarice,
the usual vices of politicians, seemed to have no place in his breast.

He seldom spoke in Congress, but was active in preparing and
doing business out of doors. . . . His abilities were considerable,
and his knowledge extensive and correct upon Revolutionary subjects, and both friends and enemies agree in viewing him as one
of the most active instruments of the American Revolution.

John Adams, of Massachusetts. He was a distant relation of
Samuel Adams, but possessed another species of character. He
had been educated a lawyer, and stood high in his profession in his
native state. He was a most sensible and forcible speaker. Every
member of Congress in 1776 acknowledged him to be the first man
in the House. Dr. Brownson (of Georgia) used to say when he
spoke, he fancied an angel was let down from heaven to illumine
the Congress. He saw the whole of a subject at a single glance, and
by a happy union of the powers of reasoning and persuasion often
succeeded in carrying measures which were at first sight of an
unpopular nature. His replies to reflections upon himself, or upon
the New England States, were replete with the most poignant
humor or satire. . . . He was equally fearless of men and of
the consequences of a bold assertion of his opinion in all his
speeches. . . .

24

John Adams

He was a stranger to dissimulation, and appeared to be more jealous of his reputation for integrity than for talents or knowledge. He was strictly moral, and at all times respectful to religion. In speaking of the probable issue of the war he said to me in Baltimore in the winter of 1777, "We shall succeed in our struggle, provided we repent of our sins, and forsake them," and then added, "I will see it out, or go to heaven in its ruins." He possessed more learning probably, both ancient and modern, than any man who subscribed the Declaration of Independence. His reading was various. Even the old English poets were familiar to him. . . . When he went to Holland to negotiate a treaty with that country, he left a blank in Congress. . . .

Stephen Hopkins, of Rhode Island. A venerable old man of the Society of Friends, of an original understanding, extensive reading, and great integrity. He perfectly understood the principles of liberty and government, and was warmly attached to the independence of his country. I once heard him say in 1776 "the liberties of America would be a cheap purchase with the loss of but 100,000 lives." He disliked hearing long letters read him from the generals of our armies, and used to say "he never knew a General Quillman good for any thing." As the result of close observation he remarked to me in walking home from Congress, that he "had never known a modest man that was not brave."

Roger Sherman, of Connecticut. A plain man of slender education. He taught himself mathematics, and afterward acquired some property and a good deal of reputation by making almanacs. He was so regular in business and so democratic in his principles that he was called by one of his friends "a republican machine."

Patrick Henry asked him in 1774 why the people of Connecticut were more zealous in the cause of liberty than the people of other states; he answered "because we have more to lose than any of them."

"What is that?" said Mr. Henry.

"Our beloved charter," replied Mr. Sherman.

He was not less distinguished for his piety than his patriotism. He once objected to a motion for Congress sitting on a Sunday upon an occasion which he thought did not require it, and gave as of the British army upon his property near New York without repining. Every attachment of his heart yielded to his love of his country.

Francis Hopkinson, of New Jersey. A facetious agreeable man. He took but a small part in the business of Congress but served his country very essentially by many of his publications during the war. . . .

Robert Morris, of Pennsylvania. A bold, sensible and agreeable speaker. His perceptions were quick and his judgment sound upon all subjects. He was opposed to the time (not to the act) of the Declaration of Independence, but he yielded to no man in his exertions to support it, and a year after it took place he publicly acknowledged on the floor of Congress that he had been mistaken in his former opinion as to its time, and said that it would have been better for our country had it been declared sooner. He was candid and liberal in a debate so as always to be respected by his opponents, and sometimes to offend the members of the party with whom he generally voted. By his extensive commercial knowledge and connections he rendered great services to his country in the beginning, and by the able manner in which he discharged the duties of financier he revived and established her credit in the close of the Revolution. In private life he was friendly, sincere, generous and charitable, but his peculiar manners deprived him of much of that popularity which usually follows great exploits of public and private virtue. He was proud and passionate, and hence he always had virulent enemies, as well as affectionate friends.

Benjamin Franklin, of Pennsylvania. He seldom spoke in Congress but was useful in committees, in which he was punctual and indefatigable. He was a firm republican, and treated kingly power at all times with ridicule and contempt. He early declared himself in favor of independence. John Adams used to say he was more of a philosopher than a politician. . . .

I sat next to him in Congress, when he was elected by the unanimous vote of every State in the Union to an embassy to the Court of France in the year 1776. When the vote was declared, I congratulated him upon it. He thanked me, and said, "I am like the remnant of a piece of unsalable cloth you may have, as the shopkeepers say, for what you please." He was then 70 years of age.

His services to his country in effecting the treaty with France

Ben Franklin and a Colleague

were highly appreciated at the time that event took place. He was treated with great respect by the French Court. A letter from Paris written while he was there contained the following expressions: "Dr. Franklin seldom goes to court. When he does he says but little, but what he says flies by the next post to every part of the Kingdom."

George Clymer, of Pennsylvania. A cool, firm, consistent republican who loved liberty and government with an equal affection. Under the appearance of manners that were cold and indolent, he concealed a mind that was always warm and active toward the interests of his country. He was well informed in history, ancient and modern, and frequently displayed flashes of wit and humor in conversation. His style in writing was simple, correct and (to use the words of Lord Peterborough when speaking of William Law) "seldom used."

Charles Carroll

Charles Carroll, of Maryland. An inflexible patriot, and an honest independent friend to his country. He had been educated at St. Omer's (the College of the English Jesuits at St. Omer, France; Charles Carroll of Carrollton studied also at Rheims, Paris, Bourges and London) and possessed considerable learning. He seldom spoke, but his speeches were sensible and correct, and delivered in an oratorical manner.

Richard Henry Lee, of Virginia. A frequent, correct and pleasing speaker. He was very useful upon committees and active in expediting business. He made the motion for the Declaration of Independence and was ever afterward one of its most zealous supporters.

Richard Henry Lee

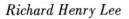

Thomas Jefferson, of Virginia. He possessed a genius of the first order. It was universal in its objects. He was not less distinguished for his political than his mathematical and philosophical knowledge. The objects of his benevolence were as extensive as those of his knowledge. He was not only the friend of his country, but of all nations and religions. While Congress were deliberating upon the measure of sending Commissioners to France I asked him what he thought of being one of them. He said "he would go to hell to serve his country." He was afterward elected a Commissioner, but declined at that time on account of the sickness of his wife. He seldom spoke in Congress.

Arthur Middleton, of South Carolina. A man of a cynical temper, but of upright intentions toward his country. He had been educated in England and was a critical Latin and Greek scholar. He read Horace and other classics during his recess from Congress. He spoke frequently, and always with asperity or personalities. He disliked business, and when put upon the Committee of Accounts he refused to serve and gave as a reason for it that "he hated accounts, that he did not even keep his own accounts, and that he knew nothing about them."

George Walton, of Georgia. A sensible young man. He possessed knowledge and a pleasing manner of speaking. He was the youngest member of Congress, being not quite three and twenty when he signed the Declaration of Independence. He filled the offices of governor and chief justice for many years in Georgia, and evinced in his public conduct the same attachment to government and order that he had done in 1776 to liberty and independence.[1]

III DEFIANCE OR RECONCILIATION

"There never appeared more perfect unity among any set of men," wrote Richard Henry Lee of Virginia about the Second Continental Congress. But that unanimity, if it ever existed, did not last very long. It was not too hard to agree on such matters as taking the army stationed near Boston under their wing, or appointing George Washington to its command, but after that members began to disagree pretty strongly. On the surface those disagreements concerned particular policies—like the proposed attack on Canada—or persons. But underneath was the fundamental question: was the Congress to work for reconciliation with Britain or for separation from Britain?

What is most interesting is that these differences were not merely between radicals like Sam Adams or Thomas Jefferson or Richard Henry Lee and conservatives like John Dickinson or John Jay or James Wilson; they were differences within the hearts and minds of individuals. Even the best of men—perhaps because they *were* the best of men—were torn by doubts and misgivings. After all there was a great deal at stake, and the decisions, as Washington himself put it, would affect "millions yet unborn." There was no clear path to follow; there was no certainty that any one policy would prove right and all others wrong. Great Britain was the greatest empire on the globe, the greatest and the most powerful. Never before in modern history had a colony broken away from a mother country. It was a solemn thing to break up the British Empire—and a dangerous one, too.

We can see something of this uncertainty and doubt in two documents from which we here give extracts: first, the Declaration of the Causes and Necessity of Taking up Arms, and second, the so-called Olive Branch Petition to the King. One justified war, the other pleaded for peace. Yet the same man, John Dickinson, was responsible for both of them—and John Adams signed both of them! To be sure Adams thought it was folly to extend an olive branch of peace at this moment—and said so in a letter which the British captured and published—but the fact is that he *did* vote for it, and so did other radical leaders like Sam Adams and Richard Henry Lee. And, just to show how even the most zealous Patriots were racked by uncertainty, consider that as late as August 25, 1776, eight weeks after he had written the Declaration, Jefferson could tell his kinsman John Randolph that he was "looking forward with fondness toward a reconciliation with Great Britain."

Actually it was George III of England who did more to help members of Congress make up their minds to independence than all the careful planning of the "brace of Adamses" or the eloquence of Patrick Henry or the literary genius of Jefferson. For when the Olive Branch Petition was sent to England, King George refused to receive it. "The King and his cabinet," wrote a member of that cabinet in a lordly way, "are determined to listen to nothing from the illegal Congress, to treat with the colonies only one by one, and in no event to recognize them in any form of association." So that was that! No wonder the French ambassador wrote home to his king that the English "appear to me in a delirium."

Had there been any encouragement from the mother country, the moderates in Congress (and out) might have gained the upper hand. But there was nothing but discouragement. Early in November 1775, Congress heard not only of the rejection of the Olive Branch Petition, but that the King had proclaimed the colonies in a state of rebellion. That was the same as a declaration of war. When British warships attacked and burned the town of Falmouth, in Maine, and word came that George III was planning to hire German mercenaries—soldiers who fought for pay—to put down the American rebellion, it was pretty hard to take reconciliation seriously.

We give here excerpts from the Declaration of the Causes and Necessity of Taking up Arms—a paper written jointly by Dickinson and Jefferson—and from the Olive Branch Petition, and with it John Adams' unfortunate letter ridiculing Dickinson for his willingness to compromise. We give, too, the Proclamation of Rebellion.

Declaration of the Causes and Necessity of Taking up Arms

July 6, 1775

. . . We are reduced to the alternative of choosing an unconditional submission to the tyranny of irritated ministers, or resistance by force. The latter is our choice. We have counted the cost of this contest, and find nothing so dreadful as voluntary slavery. Honor, justice, and humanity forbid us tamely to surrender that freedom which we received from our gallant ancestors, and which our innocent posterity have a right to receive from us. We cannot endure the infamy and guilt of resigning succeeding generations to that wretchedness which inevitably awaits them, if we basely entail hereditary bondage upon them.

Our cause is just. Our union is perfect. Our internal resources are great, and, if necessary, foreign assistance is undoubtedly attainable. We gratefully acknowledge, as signal instances of the Divine favor toward us, that His Providence would not permit us to be called into this severe controversy, until we were grown up to our present strength, had been previously exercised in warlike operation, and possessed of the means of defending ourselves. With hearts fortified with these animating reflections, we most solemnly, before God and the world, declare that, exerting the utmost energy of those powers which our beneficent Creator hath graciously bestowed upon us, the arms we have been compelled by our enemies to assume, we will, in defiance of every hazard, with unabating firmness and perseverance, employ for the preservation of our liberties; being with one mind resolved to die freemen rather than to live slaves.

Lest this declaration should disquiet the minds of our friends and fellow subjects in any part of the empire, we assure them that we mean not to dissolve that union which has so long and so happily subsisted between us, and which we sincerely wish to see restored. Necessity has not yet driven us into that desperate measure, nor induced us to excite any other nation to war against them. We have not raised armies with ambitious designs of separating from Great Britain, and establishing independent states. We fight not for glory or for conquest. We exhibit to mankind the remarkable spectacle of a people attacked by unprovoked enemies, without any imputation or even suspicion of offenses. . . .

With an humble confidence in the mercies of the supreme and impartial Judge and Ruler of the Universe, we most devoutly implore His divine goodness to protect us happily through this great conflict, to dispose our adversaries to reconciliation on reasonable terms, and thereby to relieve the empire from the calamities of civil war.

By order of Congress
JOHN HANCOCK, *President*[1]

Congress Sends an Olive Branch Petition

To the King's Most Excellent Majesty.

July 8, 1775

Most Gracious Sovereign: We, Your Majesty's faithful subjects in the Colonies.

Attached to Your Majesty's person, family and government, with all devotion that principle and affection can inspire; connected with Great Britain by the strongest ties that can unite societies, and deploring every event that tends in any degree to weaken them, we solemnly assure Your Majesty that we not only most ardently desire the former harmony between her and these Colonies may be restored, but that a concord may be established between them upon so firm a basis as to perpetuate its blessings, uninterrupted by any future dissensions to succeeding generations in both countries, and to transmit Your Majesty's name to posterity, adorned with that signal and lasting glory that has attended the memory of those illustrious personages, whose virtues and abilities have extricated states from dangerous convulsions, and by securing happiness to others have erected the most noble and durable monuments to their own fame.

We therefore beseech Your Majesty, that your loyal authority and influence may be graciously interposed to procure us relief from our afflicting fears and jealousies, occasioned by the system before-mentioned, and to settle peace through every part of our Dominions, with all humility submitting to Your Majesty's wise consideration, whether it may not be expedient, for facilitating those important purposes, that Your Majesty be pleased to direct some mode, by which the united applications of your faithful Colonists to the Throne, in pursuance of their common counsels may be improved into a happy and permanent reconciliation; and that, in the meantime, measures may be taken for preventing the further destruction of the lives of Your Majesty's subjects; and that such statutes as more immediately distress any of Your Majesty's Colonies may be repealed. . . .[2]

"Mr. Dickinson Gives a Silly Cast to Our Doings"

From the Diary of John Adams.

I took my hat, and went out of the door of Congress Hall. Mr. Dickinson observed me and darted out after me. He broke out upon me in a most abrupt and extraordinary manner: in as violent a passion as he was capable of feeling, and with an air, countenance and gestures as rough and haughty as if I had been a schoolboy and he the master. He vociferated, "What is the reason, Mr. Adams, that you New England men oppose our measures

The State House in Philadelphia, 1778

of reconciliation? There, now, is Sullivan, in a long harangue, following you in a determined opposition to our petition to the King. Look ye! If you don't concur with us in our pacific system, I and a number of us will break off from you and New England, and we will carry on the opposition by ourselves in our own way." I own I was shocked with this magisterial salutation. . . .

The more I reflected on Mr. Dickinson's rude lecture in the State House yard, the more I was vexed with it; and the determination of Congress in favor of the petition did not allay the irritation. . . . I took my pen and wrote a very few lines to my wife, and about an equal number to General James Warren. Irritated with the unpoliteness of Mr. Dickinson and more mortified with his success in Congress, I wrote something like what has been published, but not exactly.[3]

John Adams to James Warren.

Philadelphia, July 24, 1775

Dear Sir: I am determined to write freely to you this time. A certain great fortune and piddling genius whose fame has been trumpeted so loudly has given a silly cast to our whole doings. We are between hawk and buzzard. We ought to have had in our hands a month ago the whole legislative, executive and judicial of the whole continent, and have completely modeled a constitution; to have raised a naval power and opened all our ports wide; to have arrested every friend of government on the continent and held them as hostages for the poor victims in Boston, and then opened the door as wide as possible for peace and reconciliation. After this they might have petitioned, negotiated, addressed, etc., if they would. Is all this extravagant? Is it wild? Is it not the soundest policy? . . .[4]

George III Proclaims the Americans in a State of Rebellion

August 23, 1775

Whereas many of our subjects in divers parts of our Colonies and Plantations in North America, misled by dangerous and ill designing men, and forgetting the allegiance which they owe to the power that has protected and supported them; after various disorderly acts committed in disturbance of the public peace, to the obstruction of lawful commerce, and to the oppression of our loyal subjects carrying on the same; have at length proceeded to open and avowed rebellion, by arraying themselves in a hostile manner, to withstand the execution of the law, and traitorously preparing, ordering and levying war against us:

And whereas, there is reason to apprehend that such rebellion

37

King George III

hath been much promoted and encouraged by the traitorous correspondence, counsels and comfort of divers wicked and desperate persons within this realm:

To the end therefore, that none of our subjects may neglect or violate their duty through ignorance thereof, or through any doubt of the protection which the law will afford to their loyalty and zeal, we have thought fit, by and with the advice of our Privy Council, to issue our Royal Proclamation, hereby declaring, that not only all our Officers, civil and military, are obliged to exert their utmost endeavors to suppress such rebellion, and to bring the traitors to justice, but that all our subjects of this Realm, and the dominions thereunto belonging, are bound by law to be aiding and assisting in the suppression of such rebellion, and to disclose and make known all traitorous conspiracies and attempts against us, our crown and dignity;

And we do accordingly strictly charge and command all our Officers, as well civil as military, and all others our obedient and loyal subjects, to use their utmost endeavors to withstand and suppress such rebellion, and to disclose and make known all treasons and traitorous conspiracies which they shall know to be against us, our crown and dignity; and for that purpose, that they transmit to one of our principal Secretaries of State, or other proper officer, due and full information of all persons who shall be found carrying on correspondence with, or in any manner or degree aiding or abetting the persons now in open arms and rebellion against our Government, within any of our Colonies and Plantations in North America, in order to bring to condign punishment the authors, perpetrators, and abetters of such traitorous designs.

Given at our Court at St. James's the twenty-third day of August, one thousand seven hundred and seventy-five, in the fifteenth year of our reign.

GOD *save the* KING.[5]

IV THE TURN OF THE TIDE

Once George III had condemned the Americans as rebels, it was much easier for them to be just that. After November 1775, therefore, the voices of moderation were more and more drowned out by cries of defiance. But even more effective than the King's Proclamation of Rebellion was the appearance, in January of 1776, of a pamphlet called *Common Sense*, by an Englishman. The author was indeed an Englishman, but a very dissatisfied one. Thomas Paine was English born and bred, but ever since he was a young man he had been in hot water with the government—mostly because his opinions were much too extreme for that government to tolerate. Franklin had advised him to go to America, and in November 1774 he arrived in Philadelphia, got a job on a newspaper, and threw himself heart and soul into the American cause.

As he himself wrote later, "When the country into which I had just set my foot was set on fire about my ears, it was time to stir. Those who had been long settled had something to defend; those who had just come had something to pursue; and the call and the concern was equal and universal. For in a country wherein all men were once adventurers, the difference of a few years in their arrival could make none in their rights."

"It was time to stir!" Tom Paine was the kind of man who is never happy unless he is stirring things up, and he had the talent to do it. His particular talent was literary; probably no other American writer ever had the genius for putting arguments in simple but exciting words that Tom Paine had.

His first important piece of writing was an essay denouncing Negro

40

slavery. This caught the attention of Benjamin Rush (who was in on everything), and Rush persuaded Paine to give his attention to a more urgent cause—the cause of independence. Nothing pleased Tom Paine more, and within a few weeks he had dashed off a pamphlet to which Rush gave the happy name *Common Sense*.

Common Sense was published on January 9, 1776, and caught on at once. Soon it was being reprinted everywhere—in Boston and Salem, Massachusetts; in Newport and Providence, Rhode Island; in New York, and in Charleston in South Carolina; and even—with suitable omissions to avoid trouble with the law—in London itself. Within a few months it had been translated into German, French and Dutch, and was being read on the European continent as well as in America. It caught the popular fancy as has nothing before or since except *Uncle Tom's Cabin;* within three months it had sold 120,000 copies—that is comparable to a sale of 6,000,000 today!

It was, as one critic wrote, "Precisely fitted to the hour, to the spot, to the passions of men. It brushes away the tangles and cobwebs of technical debate, and flashes common sense upon the situation. It was meant for plain men, in desperate danger, and desperately in earnest." Above all it gave simple arguments in language that could be understood by everybody, and it appealed irresistibly to the growing sense of Americanism and of independence.

From all parts of the country came testimony to the effect of *Common Sense* on the hearts and minds of men. Radicals were delighted. "I beg leave to let you know that I have read *Common Sense*," wrote Major Joseph Hawley of western Massachusetts to his friend Elbridge Gerry, "and that every sentiment has sunk into my well-prepared heart." And even the cautious Washington wrote that "*Common Sense* is working a powerful change in the minds of men." Moderates and conservatives were cast down; they thought it not common sense but nonsense and dangerous nonsense at that.

We give here early sentiments for independence from Thomas Jefferson and General Nathanael Greene; Benjamin Rush's account of how *Common Sense* came to be written (with due attention to Rush's part in it!); and a series of excerpts from *Common Sense* itself.

Early Sentiments for Independence

Thomas Jefferson to John Randolph.

Philadelphia, November 29, 1775

Dear Sir: . . . It is an immense misfortune to the whole Empire, to have a King of such a disposition at such a time. We are told, and everything proves it true, that he is the bitterest enemy we have. His Majesty is able, and that satisfies me that ignorance or wickedness somewhere controls him. In an earlier part of this contest, our petitions told him that from our King there was but one appeal. The admonition was despised, and that appeal forced on us. To undo his Empire, he has but one more truth to learn: that, after Colonies have drawn the sword, there is but one step more they can take. That step is now pressed upon us, by the measures adopted, as if they were afraid we would not take it.

Believe me, dear Sir, there is not in the British Empire a man who more cordially loves a union with Great Britain than I do. But, by the God that made me, I will cease to exist before I yield to a connection on such terms as the British Parliament propose; and in this I think I speak the sentiments of America. We want neither inducement nor power, to declare and assert a separation. It is will alone which is wanting, and that is growing apace, under the fostering hand of our King. One bloody campaign will probably decide, everlastingly, our future course; I am sorry to find a bloody campaign is decided on. If our winds and waters should not combine to rescue their shores from slavery, and General Howe's re-enforcement should arrive in safety, we have hopes he will be inspirited to come out of Boston and take another drubbing; and we must drub him soundly, before the sceptered tyrant will know we are not mere brutes, to crush under his hand, and kiss the rod with which he deigns to scourge us.

Yours, &c.,

THOMAS JEFFERSON[1]

42

General Nathanael Greene to Samuel Ward, a member of Congress from Rhode Island.

Camp on Prospect Hill, January 4, 1776

Dear Sir. . . . I am now to open my mind a little more freely.

It hath been said that Canada in the late war was conquered in Germany. Who knows but that Britain may be in the present controversy! I take it for granted that France and Spain have made overtures to the Congress. Let us embrace them as brothers. We want not their land force in America: their navy we do. Their commerce will be mutually beneficial; they will doubtless pay the expense of their fleet, as it will be employed in protecting their own trade. Their military stores we want amazingly. Those will be articles of commerce. . . .

Permit me, then, to recommend from the sincerity of my heart, ready at all times to bleed in my country's cause, a declaration of independence; and call upon the world, and the great God who governs it, to witness the necessity, propriety and rectitude thereof.

My worthy friend, the interests of mankind hang upon that truly worthy body of which you are a member. You stand the representatives not of America only, but of the whole world; the friends of liberty, and the supporters of the rights of human nature.

How will posterity, millions yet unborn, bless the memory of those brave patriots who are now hastening the consummation of freedom, truth and religion! But want of decision renders wisdom in council insignificant, as want of power hath prevented us here from destroying the mercenary troops now in Boston. . . . How can we, then, startle at the idea of expense, when our whole property, our dearest connections, our liberty, nay! life itself is at stake? Let us, therefore, act like men inspired with a resolution that nothing but the frowns of Heaven shall conquer us. It is no time for deliberation; the hour is swiftly rolling on when the plains of America will be deluged with human blood. Resolves, declarations and all the parade of heroism in words will not obtain a victory. Arms and ammunition are as necessary as men and must be had at the expense of everything short of Britain's claims. . . .[2]

Dr. Rush Stands Godfather to *Common Sense*

From Dr. Rush's Autobiography.

About the year 1774 a certain Thomas Paine arrived in Philadelphia from England with a letter of recommendation from Dr. Franklin. . . . In one of my visits to Mr. Aitken's bookstore I met with Mr. Paine, and was introduced to him by Mr. Aitken. His conversation became at once interesting. I asked him to visit me, which he did a few days afterward. Our subjects of conversation were political. I perceived with pleasure that he had realized the independence of the American colonies upon Great Britain, and that he considered the measure as necessary to bring the war to a speedy and successful issue.

I had before this interview put some thoughts upon paper upon this subject, and was preparing an address to the inhabitants of the colonies upon it. But I had hesitated as to the time, and I shuddered at the prospect of the consequence of its not being well received. I mentioned the subject to Mr. Paine, and asked him what he thought of writing a pamphlet upon it. I suggested to him that he had nothing to fear from the popular odium to which such a publication might expose him, for he could live anywhere, but that my profession and connections, which tied me to Philadelphia where a great majority of the citizens and some of my friends were hostile to a separation of our country from Great Britain, forbade me to come forward as a pioneer in that important controversy. He readily assented to the proposal, and from time to time he called at my house and read to me every chapter of the proposed pamphlet as he composed it. I recollect being charmed with a sentence in it which by accident, or perhaps by design, was not published. It was as follows: "Nothing can be conceived of more absurd than three millions of people flocking to the American shore every time a vessel arrives from England, to know what portion of liberty they shall enjoy."

When Mr. Paine had finished his pamphlet, I advised him to show it to Dr. Franklin, Mr. Rittenhouse and Samuel Adams, all of whom I knew were decided friends to American independence. I mention these facts to refute a report that Mr. Paine was assisted in composing his pamphlet by one or more of the above gentlemen. They never saw it till it was written, and then only by my advice. I gave it at his request the title of "Common Sense."[3]

Excerpts from *Common Sense*

By Thomas Paine.

As much has been said of the advantages of reconciliation, which, like an agreeable dream, has passed away and left us as we were, it is but right that we should examine the contrary side of the argument, and inquire into some of the many material injuries which these colonies sustain, and always will sustain, by being connected with and dependent on Great Britain. To examine that connection and dependence on the principles of nature and common sense; to see what we have to trust to, if separated, and what we are to expect, if dependent.

I have heard it asserted by some, that as America has flourished under her former connection with Great Britain, the same connection is necessary towards her future happiness, and will always have the same effect. Nothing can be more fallacious than this kind of argument. We may as well assert that because a child has thrived upon milk, it is never to have meat, or that the first twenty years of our lives is to become a precedent for the next twenty. But even this is admitting more than is true; for I answer roundly that America would have flourished as much, and probably much more, had no European power taken any notice of her. The commerce by which she hath enriched herself are the necessaries of

45

Thomas Paine

life, and will always have a market while eating is the custom of Europe. . . .

But Britain is the parent country, say some. Then the more shame upon her conduct. Even brutes do not devour their young, nor savages make war upon their families; wherefore, the assertion, if true, turns to her reproach; but it happens not to be true, or only partly so, and the phrase *parent* or *mother country* hath been . . . adopted by the king and his parasites, with a low . . . design of gaining an unfair bias on the credulous weakness of our minds. Europe, and not England, is the parent country of America. This new world hath been the asylum for the persecuted lovers of civil and religious liberty from *every part* of Europe. Hither have they fled, not from the tender embraces of the mother, but from the cruelty of the monster; and it is so far true of England, that the same tyranny which drove the first emigrants from home pursues their descendants still. . . .

I challenge the warmest advocate for reconciliation to show a single advantage that this continent can reap by being connected with Great Britain. I repeat the challenge, not a single advantage is derived. Our corn will fetch its price in any market in Europe, and our imported goods must be paid for, buy them where we will.

But the injuries and disadvantages which we sustain by that connection are without number; and our duty to mankind at large, as well as to ourselves, instruct us to renounce the alliance: because any submission to, or dependence on, Great Britain, tends directly to involve this continent in European wars and quarrels, and set us at variance with nations who would otherwise seek our friendship, and against whom we have neither anger nor complaint. As Europe is our market for trade, we ought to form no partial connection with any part of it. 'Tis the true interest of America to steer clear of European contentions, which she never can do while by her dependence on Britain she is made the makeweight in the scale of British politics.

Europe is too thickly planted with kingdoms to be long at peace, and whenever a war breaks out between England and any foreign power, the trade of America goes to ruin, *because of her connection with Britain*. The next war may not turn out like the last, and should it not, the advocates for reconciliation now will be wishing for separation then, because neutrality in that case would be a safer convoy than a man of war. Everything that is right or reasonable pleads for separation. The blood of the slain, the weeping voice of nature cries, *'Tis time to part*. Even the distance at which the Almighty hath placed England and America is a strong and natural proof that the authority of the one over the other was never the design of heaven. . . .

It is repugnant to reason, to the universal order of things, to all examples from former ages, to suppose that this continent can long remain subject to any external power. The most sanguine in Britain doth not think so. The utmost stretch of human wisdom cannot, at this time, compass a plan, short of separation, which can promise the continent even a year's security. Reconciliation is *now* a fallacious dream. Nature has deserted the connection, and art cannot supply her place. For, as Milton wisely expresses, "Never can true reconcilement grow where wounds of deadly hate have pierced so deep." . . .

As to government matters, it is not in the power of Britain to do this continent justice: the business of it will soon be too weighty and intricate to be managed with any tolerable degree of convenience by a power so distant from us, and so very ignorant of us; for if they cannot conquer us they cannot govern us. To be always running three or four thousand miles with a tale or a petition, waiting four or five months for an answer, which, when obtained, requires five or six more to explain it in, will in a few years be looked upon as folly and childishness. There was a time when it was proper, and there is a proper time for it to cease. . . .

48

Small islands not capable of protecting themselves are the proper objects for government to take under their care; but there is something absurd in supposing a continent to be perpetually governed by an island. In no instance hath nature made the satellite larger than its primary planet; and as England and America, with respect to each other, reverse the common order of nature, it is evident that they belong to different systems. England to Europe: America to itself.

I am not induced by motives of pride, party, or resentment to espouse the doctrine of separation and independence; I am clearly, positively, and conscientiously persuaded that 'tis the true interest of this continent to be so; that everything short of *that* is mere patchwork, that it can afford no lasting felicity—that it is leaving the sword to our children, and shrinking back at a time when a little more, a little further, would have rendered this continent the glory of the earth. . . .

To talk of friendship with those in whom our reason forbids us to have faith, and our affections wounded through a thousand pores instruct us to detest, is madness and folly. Every day wears out the little remains of kindred between us and them; and can there be any reason to hope that as the relationship expires the affection will increase, or that we shall agree better when we have ten times more and greater concerns to quarrel over than ever?

Ye that tell us of harmony and reconciliation, can ye restore to us the time that is past? . . . Neither can ye reconcile Britain and America. The last cord now is broken, the people of England are presenting addresses against us. There are injuries which nature cannot forgive; she would cease to be nature if she did. . . . The continent cannot forgive the murderers of Britain. The Almighty hath implanted in us these inextinguishable feelings for good and wise purposes. They are the guardians of his image in our hearts. They distinguish us from the herd of common animals. The social compact would dissolve, and justice be extirpated from the earth, or have only a casual existence, were we callous to the touches of affection. The robber and the murderer would often escape unpunished, did not the injuries which our tempers sustain, provoke us into justice.

O ye that love mankind! Ye that dare oppose not only the tyranny but the tyrant, stand forth! Every spot of the old world is overrun with oppression. Freedom hath been hunted round the globe. Asia and Africa have long expelled her. Europe regards her like a stranger, and England hath given her warning to depart. O receive the fugitive, and prepare in time an asylum for mankind![4]

V INDEPENDENCE LIKE A TORRENT

By the spring of 1776 the current was flowing swiftly toward independence. General Washington had chased the British from Boston, and this stunning victory was partly responsible for the new note of confidence. Partly responsible, too, was the immense popularity of *Common Sense,* which showed the way the wind was blowing. And finally there was the growing realization that the policy of George III left Americans no genuine alternatives but submission or separation— and it was too late now to talk of submission.

In any event, during the winter and early-spring months, the Continental Congress took one bold and decisive step after another toward independence. On January 2 it voted to disarm all Loyalists—all those, that is, who looked as if they might support the mother country on the issue of independence. On March 1 it decided to send Silas Deane, of Connecticut, to France to get such help as he could from the French king, and told him to spread the word that there was every likelihood that the American colonies would soon "come to a total separation." That is what the French were waiting to hear, and they responded at once (though secretly) with money and supplies. Later in March the Congress armed private merchant vessels and permitted them to prey on British commerce. On April 6 the ports were opened to trade with all countries except Britain.

Even more important was the swift change of sentiment in the states, for after all it was the states that would decide, in the end, what Congress did about independence. Almost everywhere, except in the Middle States, those who favored separation succeeded in getting control of the machinery of government and committing their states to independence. As early as March 26, South Carolina adopted a state constitution—an act which was, in itself, a gesture of independence. On April 12 her sister state of North Carolina took the bold step of definitely instructing her delegates in Congress to vote for independence. Early in May, Rhode Island followed her lead.

Everything really depended on Massachusetts and Virginia. They had taken the lead in the struggle against the mother country and, in men like Samuel and John Adams and James Warren, like Washington and Jefferson and Patrick Henry, they had furnished the leaders, too. Now at last they pushed things to their logical conclusion: independence. On May 10 the Provisional Government of Massachusetts voted to sound out public opinion in that state: they asked the towns to decide whether they were ready for independence. All through May and June the freemen of Massachusetts—every man over twenty-one— met in town meetings and solemnly debated the great question. Here and there some moderates sounded a warning note, but they were always voted down. In the end every town in Massachusetts voted for independence. That was democracy with a vengeance: in no other country in the world would a major question of this kind have been submitted to public debate and decision!

Next, Virginia. There the dunderheaded royal governor, Lord Dunmore, had managed to antagonize all his own supporters, and to drive all moderates into the radical camp. When a convention met at the little capitol in Williamsburg, on May 6, support for independence was all but unanimous. The question was not, in fact, whether it would vote for separation—there was never any doubt about that—but just how it would do so: whether by its own independent act, or by acting through the Continental Congress. In the end Virginians decided to act through Congress, and on May 15 a resolution calling on the Congress to vote independence passed unanimously. That night the old capitol was illuminated with bonfires and torches, while excited Patriots paraded, rang church bells, fired salutes and hauled down

George Washington

the British flag and raised a "Union Flag of the American States."

The Virginia resolutions did not reach Philadelphia until the end of May; meantime Congress itself, fully aware of the tide of public opinion, took a decisive step. Early that month John Adams introduced a resolution instructing every colony to adopt a new government "such as shall best conduce to the happiness and safety of their constituents in particular and America in general." What this meant was that every state should do what South Carolina had done—write a constitution and form a government, a step which would make it an independent state rather than a colony. This fateful resolution was adopted on May 10, and five days later—just as Virginia was acting—Congress added a preamble to the resolution, which was a sort of trial run on independence: "It is necessary," said the preamble, "that the exercise of every kind of authority under the Crown should be totally suppressed." That night John Adams wrote triumphantly to his wife that "Great Britain has at last driven America to the last step, a complete separation from her; a total absolute independence."

All our witnesses here are old friends by now: the Massachusetts contingent, Sam and John Adams and their friends James Warren, Elbridge Gerry and Joseph Hawley. We include here, too, some samples (out of scores) of resolutions by Massachusetts towns. Not many country towns today, it is safe to say, could draw up resolutions so powerful and so eloquent.

"Trust Our Cause to Our Swords"

Samuel Adams to James Warren.

Philadelphia, April 16, 1776

My Dear Sir,—I have not yet congratulated you on the unexpected and happy change of our affairs in the removal of the rebel army from Boston. Our worthy friend Major Hawley in his letter to me declines giving me joy on this occasion. He thinks it best to put off the ceremony till the Congress shall proclaim Independency. In my opinion, however, it becomes us to rejoice and religiously to acknowledge the goodness of the Supreme Being who in this instance hath signally appeared for us. Our countrymen are too wise to suffer this favorable event to put them off their guard. They will fortify the harbor of Boston, still defend the sea coasts and keep the military spirit universally alive.

I perfectly agree with the major in his opinion of the necessity of proclaiming Independency. The salvation of this country depends upon its being done speedily. I am anxious to have it done. Every day's delay tries my patience. I can give you not the least color of a reason why it is not done. We are told that Commissioners are coming out to offer us such terms of reconciliation as we may with safety accept of. Why then should we shut the door? This is all amusement. I am exceedingly disgusted when I hear it mentioned. Experience should teach us to pay no regard to it. We know that it has been the constant practice of the King and his junto ever since this struggle began to endeavor to make us believe their designs were pacific, while they have been meditating the most destructive plans, and they insult our understandings by attempting thus to impose upon us even while they are putting these plans into execution.

Can the King repeal or dispense with Acts of Parliament? Would he repeal the detestable Acts which we have complained of, if it was in his power? Did he ever show a disposition to do acts of justice and redress the grievances of his subjects? Why then do gentlemen expect it? They do not scruple to own that he is a tyrant; are they then willing to be his slaves and dependent upon a nation so lost to all sense of liberty and virtue as to enable and encourage him to act the tyrant? This has been done by the British nation against the remonstrances of common honesty and common sense. They are now doing it and will continue to do it, until we break the band of connection and publicly avow an independence.

It is folly for us to suffer ourselves any longer to be amused. Reconciliation upon reasonable terms is no part of their plan: the only alternative is independence or slavery. Their designs still are as they ever have been to subjugate us. Our unalterable resolution should be to be free. They have attempted to subdue us by force, but God be praised! in vain. Their arts may be more dangerous than their arms. Let us then renounce all treaty with them upon any score but that of total separation, and under God trust our cause to our swords.

. . . There are moderate men here, but their principles are daily going out of fashion. The child Independence is now struggling for birth. I trust that in a short time it will be brought forth and in spite of Pharaoh all America shall hail the dignified stranger.[1]

"Let There Be a Full Revolution"

Joseph Hawley to Elbridge Gerry.

Watertown, May 1, 1776

My Dear Sir,

The Tories dread a declaration of independency and a course of conduct on that plan more than death. They console themselves with a belief that the southern colonies will not accede to it. My hand and heart is full of it. There will be no abiding union without it. When the colonies come to be pressed with taxes they will divide and crumble to pieces. Will a government stand on recommendations? They will not. Can we subsist, and support our trading people without trade? It appears more and more every day in the country and the army that we cannot. Nay, without a real continental government our army will overrun us, and people will by and by, sooner than you may be aware of, call for their old constitutions, and as they did in England after Cromwell's death, call in Charles the Second. For God's sake let there be a full revolution, or all has been done in vain. Independence and a well planned continental government will save us. God bless you. Amen and amen. J.H.[2]

"A Final Declaration Is Approaching"

Elbridge Gerry to James Warren.

Philadelphia, May 20, 1776

In this colony [Pennsylvania] the spirit of the people is great, if a judgment is to be formed by appearances. They are well convinced of the injury their assembly has done to the continent by their instructions to their delegates. It was these instructions which included the Middle Colonies, and some of the Southern, to backward every measure which had the appearance of Independency. To them is owing the delay of Congress in agitating questions of the greatest importance, which long ere now must have terminated in a separation from Great Britain. To them is owing the disadvantages we now experience, for want of a full supply of every necessary for carrying on the war. Alliances might have been formed, and a diversion been given to the enemy's arms in Europe or the West Indies, had these instructions never appeared. But they had their effect; and while we endeavor to recover the Continent from the ill consequences of such feeble politics, we ought to show the cause of such miserable policy. It appears to me that the eyes of every unbeliever are now open; that all are sensible of the perfidy of Great Britain, and are convinced there is no medium between unqualified submission and actual Independency. The colonies are determined on the latter. A final declaration is approaching with great rapidity. May the all-wise Disposer of events so direct our affairs that they may terminate in the salvation of these afflicted colonies! . . .[3]

"Every Day Rolls in upon Us Independence like a Torrent"

John Adams to James Warren.

May 20, 1776

My Dear Sir,—Every post and every day rolls in upon us Independence like a torrent. The delegates from Georgia made their appearance this day in Congress with unlimited powers and these gentlemen themselves are very firm. South Carolina has erected her government and given her delegates ample powers, and they are firm enough. North Carolina have given theirs full powers, after repealing an instruction given last August against Confederation and Independence. This day's post has brought a multitude of letters from Virginia, all of which breathe the same spirit. They agree they shall institute a government—all are agreed in this, they say. Here are four colonies to the southward who are perfectly agreed now with the four to the northward. Five in the middle are not yet quite so ripe; but they are very near it. I expect that New York will come to a fresh election of delegates in the course of this week, give them full powers, and determine to institute a government.

The Convention of New Jersey is about meeting and will assume a government.

Pennsylvania Assembly meets this day and it is said will repeal their instruction to their delegates which has made them so exceedingly obnoxious to America in general, and their own constituents in particular.

We have had an entertaining maneuver this morning in the State House yard. The Committee of the City summoned a meeting at nine o'clock in the State House yard to consider of the Resolve of Congress of the fifteenth instant. The weather was very rainy, and the meeting was in the open air like the Comitia of the Romans; a stage was erected *extempore* for the moderator and the few orators to ascend—Colonel Roberdeau was the Moderator; Colonel McKean, Colonel Cadwallader and Colonel Matlack the principal orators. It was the very first town meeting I ever saw in Philadelphia and it was conducted with great order, decency and propriety.

The first step taken was this: the Moderator produced the Resolve of Congress of the 15th instant and read it with a loud stentorian voice that might be heard a quarter of a mile. "Whereas his Britannic Majesty, etc." As soon as this was read, the multitude, several thousands, some say, though so wet, rended the welkin with three cheers, hats flying as usual, etc.

Then a number of resolutions were produced, and moved, and determined with great unanimity. These resolutions I will send you as soon as published. The drift of the whole was that the Assembly was not a body properly constituted, authorized, and qualified to carry the resolve for instituting a new government into execution and therefore that a Convention should be called. And at last they voted to support and defend the measure of a Convention, at the utmost hazard and at all events, etc.

The Delaware Government, generally, is of the same opinion with the best Americans, very orthodox in their faith and very exemplary in their practice. Maryland remains to be mentioned. That is so eccentric a colony—sometimes so hot, sometimes so cold; now so high, then so low—that I know not what to say about it or to expect from it. I have often wished it could exchange places with Halifax. When they get agoing I expect some wild extravagant flight or other from it. To be sure they must go beyond everybody else when they begin to go.

Thus I have rambled through the continent, and you will perceive by this state of it, that we can't be very remote from the most decisive measures and the most critical events. What do you think must be my sensations when I see the Congress now daily passing resolutions which I most earnestly pressed for against wind and tide twelve months ago? and which I have not omitted to labor for a month together from that time to this? What do you think must be my reflections when I see the Farmer Dickinson himself now confessing the falsehood of all his prophecies, and the truth of mine, and confessing himself now for instituting governments, forming a Continental Constitution, making alliances with foreigners, opening ports and all that—and confessing that the defense of the colonies and preparations for defense have been neglected, in consequence of fond delusive hopes and deceitful expectations?

I assure you this is no gratification of my vanity.

The gloomy prospect of carnage and devastation that now presents itself in every part of the continent, and which has been in the most express and decisive, nay dogmatical terms foretold by me a thousand times, is too affecting to give me pleasure. It moves my keenest indignation. Yet I dare not hint at these things for I hate to give pain to gentlemen whom I believe sufficiently punished by their own reflections.[4]

Massachusetts Town Meetings Call for Independence

Malden Declares Why Independence Is Necessary

At a legal meeting of the inhabitants of the town of Malden (Mass.), May 27, 1776, it was voted unanimously that the following instructions be given to their representative, viz. to Mr. Ezra Sargeant.

Sir—A resolution of the hon. house of representatives, calling upon the several towns in this colony to express their minds in respect to the important question of American independence, is the occasion of our now instructing you. The time was, sir, when we loved the king and the people of Great Britain with an affection truly filial; we felt ourselves interested in their glory; we shared in their joys and sorrows; we cheerfully poured the fruit of all our labors into the lap of our mother country, and without reluctance expended our blood and our treasure in their cause.

These were our sentiments toward Great Britain while she continued to act the part of a parent state; we felt ourselves happy in our connection with her, nor wished it to be dissolved; but our sentiments are altered, it is now the ardent wish of our soul that America may become a free and independent state.

A sense of unprovoked injuries will arouse the resentment of the most peaceful. Such injuries these colonies have received from Britain. Unjustifiable claims have been made by the king and his minions to tax us without our consent; these claims have been prosecuted in a manner cruel and unjust to the highest degree. The frantic policy of administration hath induced them to send fleets and armies to America; that, by depriving us of our trade, and cutting the throats of our brethren, they might awe us into submission and erect a system of despotism in America, which should so far enlarge the influence of the crown as to enable it to rivet their shackles upon the people of Great Britain.

This plan was brought to a crisis upon the ever memorable nineteenth of April. We remember the fatal day! the expiring groans of our countrymen yet vibrate on our ears! and we now behold the flames of their peaceful dwellings ascending to Heaven! We hear their blood crying to us from the ground for vengeance, charging us, as we value the peace of their names, to have no further connection with [their murderers]. Who can unfeelingly hear of their slaughter and composedly sleep with their blood upon his soul? The manner in which the war has been prosecuted hath confirmed us in these sentiments; piracy and murder, robbery and breach of faith, have been conspicuous in the conduct of the king's troops: defenseless towns have been attacked and destroyed: the ruins of Charlestown, which are daily in our view, daily remind of this: the cries of the widow and the orphan demand our attention; they demand that the hand of pity should wipe the tear from their eye, and that the sword of their country should avenge their wrongs.

We long entertained hope that the spirit of the British nation would once more induce them to assert their own and our rights, and bring to condign punishment the elevated villains who have trampled upon the sacred rights of men and affronted the majesty of the people. We hoped in vain; they have lost their love to freedom, they have lost their spirit of just resentment; we therefore renounce with disdain our connection with a kingdom of slaves; we bid a final adieu to Britain. . . .

For these reasons, as well as many others which might be produced, we are confirmed in the opinion that the present age would be deficient in their duty to God, their posterity and themselves, if they do not establish an American republic. This is the only form of government which we wish to see established; for we can never be willingly subject to any other King than he who, being possessed of infinite wisdom, goodness and rectitude, is alone fit to possess unlimited power.[5]

Scituate Townsmen Pledge Their Lives to Independence

Instructions to Nathan Cushing, Esqr., Representative of the Town of Scituate.

June 4, 1776

The inhabitants of this town being called together on the recommendation of our General Assembly to signify your minds on the great point of Independence on Great Britain, think fit to instruct you on that head.

The Ministry of that Kingdom, having formed a design of subjecting the colonies to a distant, external and absolute power in all cases whatsoever, wherein the colonies have not, nor in the nature of things can have any share by representation, have, for a course of years past, exerted their utmost art and endeavor to put the same plan, so destructive to both countries, into execution. But finding it, through the noble and virtuous opposition of the Sons of Freedom, impracticable by means of mere political artifice and corruption, they have at length had a fatal recourse to a standing army, so repugnant to the nature of a free government, to fire and sword, to bloodshed and devastation, calling in the aid of foreign troops, as well as endeavoring to stir up the savages of the wilderness to exercise their barbarities upon us, being determined, by all appearances, if practicable, to extirpate the Americans from the face of the earth, unless they tamely resign the rights of humanity, and to repeople this once happy country with the ready sons of vassalage, if such can be found.

We therefore, apprehending such a subjection utterly incon-

62

sistent with the just rights and blessings of society, unanimously instruct you to endeavor that our delegates in Congress be informed, in case that representative body of the continent should think fit to declare the colonies independent of Great Britain, of our readiness and determination to assist with our Lives and Fortunes in support of that, we apprehend, necessary measure.[6]

Massachusetts Is "United on This Great Question"

James Warren to Elbridge Gerry.

Watertown, June 12, 1776

You have, no doubt, seen in the papers a short resolve, passed at the close of the last session, for the purpose of getting the sense of the whole country, by the instructions given to their members on the subject of independence. The members have severally been called on by the House, and more than one half of them are instructed fully in favor of it, and not one against it. Many more are expecting similar instructions to follow them, and near or perhaps all would have had them, if the resolve had reached them in season. Thus it appears to me the sentiments of our colony are more united on this great question than they ever were on any other; perhaps ninety-nine in a hundred would engage, with their lives and fortunes, to support Congress in the measure. You seem to intend to avoid too great a shock; there is little left to do but the form and ceremony, but even that is important; your resolves for trade and captures, and your resolve for assuming government, the preamble of which is extremely grand, make the substance of the thing.[7]

Virginia Resolves for Independence

In Convention, May the 15th, 1776
Present One Hundred and Twelve Members
Forasmuch as all the endeavors of the United Colonies by the

most decent representations and petitions to the king and parliament of Great Britain to restore peace and security to America under the British government and a reunion with that people upon just and liberal terms instead of a redress of grievances have produced from an imperious and vindictive administration increased insult, oppression and a vigorous attempt to effect our total destruction. By a late act, all these colonies are declared to be in rebellion and out of the protection of the British crown, our properties subjected to confiscation, our people, when captivated, compelled to join in the murder and plunder of their relations and countrymen, and all former rapine and oppression of Americans declared legal and just. Fleets and armies are raised, and the aid of foreign troops engaged to assist these destructive purposes. The king's representative in this colony hath not only withheld all the powers of government from operating for our safety, but, having retired on board an armed ship, is carrying on a piratical and savage war against us, tempting our slaves by every artifice to resort to him, and training and employing them against their masters. In this state of extreme danger, we have no alternative left but an abject submission to the will of those overbearing tyrants, or a total separation from the crown and government of Great Britain, uniting and exerting the strength of all America for defense, and forming alliances with foreign powers for commerce and aid in war:

Wherefore, appealing to the SEARCHER OF HEARTS for the sincerity of former declarations, expressing our desire to preserve the connection with that nation, and that we are driven from that inclination by their wicked councils, and the eternal laws of self-preservation:

RESOLVED unanimously, that the delegates appointed to represent this colony in General Congress be instructed to propose to that respectable body to declare the United Colonies free and independent states, absolved from all allegiance to, or dependence upon, the crown or parliament of Great Britain; and that they give the assent of this colony to such declaration, and to whatever measures may be thought proper and necessary by the Congress for forming foreign alliances and a confederation of the colonies, at such time, and in such manner, as to them shall seem best; *Provided,* that the power of forming government for, and the regulations of the internal concerns of each colony, be left to the respective colonial legislatures.

RESOLVED unanimously, that a committee be appointed to prepare a *Declaration of Rights,* and such a plan of government as will be most likely to maintain peace and order in this colony, and secure substantial and equal liberty to the people.

EDMUND PENDLETON, President[8]

Recommendations by the Congress to Establish New Governments

In Congress, May 15, 1776

Whereas his Britannic Majesty, in conjunction with the Lords and Commons of Great Britain, has, by a late act of Parliament, excluded the inhabitants of these United Colonies from the protection of his Crown: And *whereas* no answer whatever to the humble petition of the Colonies for redress of grievances and reconciliation with Great Britain has been, or is likely to be, given; but the whole force of that Kingdom, aided by foreign mercenaries, is to be exerted for the destruction of the good people of these Colonies: And *whereas* it appears absolutely irreconcilable to reason and good conscience for the people of these colonies now to take the oaths and affirmations necessary for the support of any government under the Crown of Great Britain; and it is necessary that the exercise of every kind of authority under the said Crown should be totally suppressed, and all the powers of government exerted under the authority of the people of the Colonies, for the preservation of internal peace, virtue, and good order, as well as for the defense of their lives, liberties and properties, against the hostile invasions and cruel depredations of their enemies: Therefore

Resolved, That it be recommended to the respective assemblies and conventions of the United Colonies, where no government sufficient to the exigencies of their affairs has been hitherto established, to adopt such government as shall, in the opinion of the representatives of the people, best conduce to the happiness and safety of their constituents in particular and America in general.

By Order of Congress, JOHN HANCOCK, *President*[9]

VI   THE FINAL DEBATE

"Not choice but necessity" dictated independence, said Richard Henry Lee, and five days later, on June 7, 1776, he introduced three momentous resolutions. The first called for a declaration of independence; the second for foreign alliances; and the third for a firm confederation of American states. These bold proposals—particularly that for independence—brought on a spirited discussion. Soon it was clear that though the majority of the state delegations in Congress were in favor of independence, the Middle States—New York, New Jersey, Pennsylvania, Delaware and Maryland—were not ready or, as one member put it, "were not yet ripe for bidding adieu to the British connection." Clearly that would never do: a United States without the five Middle States was unthinkable. Besides, as sage old Benjamin Franklin had put it, "we must all hang together or we shall hang separately." So it was agreed to postpone action on the independence resolution for three weeks: time enough for the states to be heard from.

That three-week delay was fatal for the conservatives who still wanted to cling to the British connection. One by one the states fell into line. There never had been any doubt about New England, and on June 14 Connecticut voted for independence, and the next day New Hampshire followed. Then came the first break in the Middle States. Delaware voted to instruct her delegates to go along with independence; and New Jersey ousted her Loyalist governor, William Franklin (son of Benjamin Franklin!) and sent a new "independence" delegation to Congress. On June 28 Maryland swung into line.

Not only was the barrier of the Middle States broken; only Pennsylvania and New York now held out!

There had already been some discussion of the Lee resolution for independence when it was first introduced, but Congress did not get to it in a formal way until July 1. Then there was a brief but heated debate. John Adams thought it was a waste of time, for "nothing was said but what had been repeated a hundred times, for six months past." But Adams was wrong. The debate cleared the air. John Dickinson, leader of the moderates, pleaded for delay, but Adams and Lee overwhelmed him with arguments for immediate action—or so they thought! Yet the vote on that day was disappointing. New Jersey and Maryland, to be sure, finally joined the independence party. But Pennsylvania still voted against independence. So, too, surprisingly enough, did South Carolina. Delaware had instructed for independence, but her new delegates had not yet arrived, so her vote was evenly divided. And New York, where a struggle for power was going on, did not vote at all. That meant only nine votes for independence, and nine out of thirteen simply wasn't enough: It had to be unanimous.

That night the patriots worked with redoubled energy to convert opponents and swing over the timid and the hesitant. McKean of Pennsylvania had already sent off a messenger to Caesar Rodney of Delaware, and, riding all night, Rodney covered the eighty miles between Dover and Philadelphia in time to swing Delaware's vote to independence. The delegates from South Carolina changed their minds overnight and ranged themselves alongside their neighbors. That made eleven states for independence; as New York was not voting, everything depended on Pennsylvania. Dickinson and his friend Robert Morris (he was later to manage the finances of the Revolution) gave up the struggle and stayed home, James Wilson (*he* was later to be Justice of the Supreme Court) changed his mind, and Pennsylvania swung into line. So on July 2—the day we *should* celebrate—Congress voted "unanimously" for independence. The decree had gone forth, as John Adams exultantly wrote, "that a more

Congress Voting Independence

equal liberty than has prevailed in other parts of the earth must be established in America."

John Adams and Thomas Jefferson are easily our best historians of independence, and we call on them here to tell the story. From Jefferson we have a lively record of the debate in Congress—a record written within a month or two of the debate itself. From Adams we have what is even better—a stream of letters which tell us not only a great deal about what was happening in Philadelphia, but also about that slightly ridiculous, energetic, excitable, lovable and quite irresistible figure, John Adams.

69

Richard Henry Lee Introduces Some Fateful Resolutions

June 7, 1776

RESOLVED, That these United Colonies are, and of right ought to be, free and independent States, that they are absolved from all allegiance to the British Crown, and that all political connection between them and the State of Great Britain is, and ought to be totally dissolved.

That it is expedient forthwith to take the most effectual measures for forming foreign Alliances.

That a plan of confederation be prepared and transmitted to the respective Colonies for their consideration and approbation.[1]

Jefferson Records the Great Debate over Independence

Notes of Proceedings in the Continental Congress.

June 7 to August 1, 1776

Friday, June 7, 1776, the Delegates from Virginia moved in obedience to instructions from their constituents that the Congress should declare that these United colonies are & of right ought to be free & independent states, that they are absolved from all allegiance to the British crown, and that all political connection between them and the state of Great Britain is & ought to be totally dissolved; that measures should be immediately taken for procuring the assistance of foreign powers, and a Confederation be formed to bind the colonies more closely together.

The house being obliged to attend at that time to some other business, the proposition was referred to the next day when the members were ordered to attend punctually at ten o'clock.

Saturday, June 8, they proceeded to take it into consideration and referred to a committee of the whole, into which they immediately resolved themselves, and passed that day & Monday the 10th in debating on the subject.

It was argued by Wilson, Robert R. Livingston, E. Rutledge, Dickinson and others:

That tho' they were friends to the measures themselves, and saw the impossibility that we should ever again be united with Gr. Britain, yet they were against adopting them at this time:

That the conduct we had formerly observed was wise & proper now, of deferring to take any capital step till the voice of the people drove us into it:

That they were our power, & without them our declarations could not be carried into effect:

That the people of the middle colonies (Maryland, Delaware, Pennsylva., the Jersies & N. York) were not yet ripe for bidding adieu to British connection but that they were fast ripening & in a short time would join in the general voice of America:

That the resolution entered into by this house on the 15th of May for suppressing the exercise of all powers derived from the crown, had shewn, by the ferment into which it had thrown these middle colonies, that they had not yet accommodated their minds to a separation from the mother country:

That some of them had expressly forbidden their delegates to consent to such a declaration, and others had given no instructions, & consequently no powers, to give such consent:

That if the delegates of any particular colony had no power to declare such colony independent, certain they were the others could not declare it for them; the colonies as yet being perfectly independent of each other:

That the assembly of Pennsylvania was now sitting above stairs, their convention would sit within a few days, the convention of New York was now sitting, & those of the Jersies and Delaware counties would meet on the Monday following & it was probable these bodies would take up the question of Independence & would declare to their delegates the voice of their state:

That if such a declaration should now be agreed to, these delegates must retire & possibly their colonies might secede from the Union:

That such a secession would weaken us more than could be compensated by any foreign alliance:

That in the event of such a division, foreign powers would either refuse to join themselves to our fortunes, or having us so much in their power as that desperate declaration would place us, they would insist on terms proportionably more hard & prejudicial:

That we had little reason to expect an alliance with those to whom alone as yet we had cast our eyes:

That France & Spain had reason to be jealous of that rising power which would one day certainly strip them of all their American possessions:

That it was more likely they should form a connection with the British court, who, if they should find themselves unable otherwise to extricate themselves from their difficulties, would agree to a partition of our territories, restoring Canada to France, & the Floridas to Spain, to accomplish for themselves a recovery of these colonies: . . .

On the other side it was urged by J. Adams, Wythe and others:

That no gentleman had argued against the policy of the right of separation from Britain, nor had supposed it possible we should ever renew our connection: that they had only opposed it's being now declared:

That the question was not whether, by a declaration of independence, we should make ourselves what we are not; but whether we should declare a fact which already exists:

That as to the people or parliament of England, we had alwais been independent of them, their restraints on our trade deriving efficacy from our acquiescence only & not from any rights they possessed of imposing them, & that so far our connection had been federal only, & was now dissolved by the commencement of hostilities:

That as to the king, we had bound to him by allegiance, but that this bond was now dissolved by his assent to the late act of parliament, by which he declares us out of his protection; and by his levying war on us, a fact which had long ago proved us out of his protection; it being a certain position in law that allegiance & protection are reciprocal, the one ceasing when the other is withdrawn: . . .

That the delegates from the Delaware counties having declared their constituents ready to join, there are only two colonies, Pennsylvania & Maryland whose delegates are absolutely tied up, and that these had by their instructions only reserved a right of confirming or rejecting the measure:

That the instructions from Pennsylvania might be accounted for from the times in which they were drawn, near a twelvemonth ago, since which the face of affairs has totally changed: . . .

That the people wait for us to lead the way:

That they are in favour of the measure, tho' the instructions given by some of their *representatives* are not:

That the voice of the representatives is not alwais consonant with the voice of the people, and that this is remarkably the case in these middle colonies:

That the effect of the resolution of the 15th. of May has proved this, which, raising the murmurs of some in the colonies of Pennsylvania & Maryland, called forth the opposing voice of the freer part of the people, & proved them to be the majority, even in these colonies:

That the backwardness of these two colonies might be ascribed partly to the influence of proprietary power & connections, & partly to their having not yet been attacked by the enemy:

That these causes were not likely to be soon removed, as there seemed no probability that the enemy would make either of these the seat of this summer's war:

That it would be in vain to wait either weeks or months for perfect unanimity, since it was impossible that all men should ever become of one sentiment on any question: . . .

That a declaration of Independence alone could render it consistent with European delicacy for European powers to treat with us, or even to receive an Ambassador from us:

That till this they would not receive our vessels into their ports, nor acknowledge the adjudications of our courts of Admiralty to be legitimate, in cases of capture of British vessels:

That tho' France & Spain may be jealous of our rising power, they must think it will be much more formidable with the addition of Great Britain; and will therefore see it their interest to prevent a coalition; but should they refuse, we shall be but where we are; whereas without trying we shall never know whether they will aid us or not:

That the present campaign may be unsuccessful, & therefore we had better propose an alliance while our affairs wear a hopeful aspect:

That to wait the event of this campaign will certainly work delay, because during this summer France may assist us effectually by cutting off those supplies of provisions from England & Ireland on which the enemy's armies here are to depend; or by setting in motion the great power they have collected in the West Indies, & calling our enemy to the defence of the possessions they have there:

That it would be idle to lose time in settling the terms of alliance, till we had first determined we would enter into alliance:

That it is necessary to lose no time in opening a trade for our people, who will want clothes, and will want money too for the paiment of taxes:

And that the only misfortune is that we did not enter into alliance with France six months sooner, as besides opening their ports for the vent of our last year's produce, they might have marched an army into Germany and prevented the petty princes there from selling their unhappy subjects to subdue us.[2]

"The Decree Is Gone Forth"

John Adams to Patrick Henry.

Philadelphia, June 3, 1776

My Dear Sir,—

. . . The dons, the bashaws, the grandees, the patricians, the sachems, the nabobs, call them by what names you please, sigh and groan and fret, and sometimes stamp and foam and curse, but all in vain. The decree is gone forth, and it cannot be recalled, that a more equal liberty than has prevailed in other parts of the earth must be established in America. The exuberance of pride which has produced an insolent domination in a few, a very few, opulent, monopolizing families, will be brought down nearer to the confines of reason and moderation than they have been used to. This is all the evil which they themselves will endure. It will do them good in this world, and in every other. For pride was not made for man, only as a tormentor.[3]

"The Most Complete Revolution in History"

John Adams to William Cushing.

Philadelphia, June 9, 1776

. . . Objects of the most stupendous magnitude, and measures in which the lives and liberties of millions yet unborn are intimately interested, are now before us. We are in the very midst of a revolution the most complete, unexpected and remarkable of any in the history of nations. A few important subjects must be dispatched before I can return to my family. Every colony must be induced to institute a perfect government. All the colonies must confederate together in some solemn band of union. The Congress must declare the colonies free and independent States, and ambassadors must be sent abroad to foreign courts to solicit their acknowledgment of us as sovereign states, and to form with them, at least with some of them, commercial treaties of friendship and alliance. When these things are once completed, I shall think that I have answered the end of my creation . . . return to my farm, family, ride circuits, plead law, or judge causes, just which you please.[4]

The Advantages of a Declaration

John Adams to John Winthrop.

Philadelphia, June 23, 1776

Your favor of June 1st is before me. It is now universally acknowledged that we are and must be independent. But still, objections are made to a declaration of it. It is said that such a declaration will arouse and unite Great Britain. But are they not already aroused and united, as much as they will be? Will not such a declaration arouse and unite the friends of liberty, the few who are left, in opposition to the present system? . . .

The advantages which will result from such a declaration are, in my opinion, very numerous and very great. After that event the colonies will hesitate no longer to complete their governments. They will establish tests, and ascertain the criminality of Toryism. The presses will produce no more seditious or traitorous speculations. Slanders upon public men and measures will be lessened. The legislatures of the colonies will exert themselves to manufacture saltpeter, sulphur, powder, arms, cannon, mortars, clothing and everything necessary for the support of life. Our civil governments will feel a vigor hitherto unknown. Our military operations by sea and land will be conducted with greater spirit. Privateers will swarm in vast numbers. Foreigners will then exert themselves to supply us with what we want. A foreign court will not disdain to treat with us upon equal terms. Nay farther, in my opinion, such a declaration, instead of uniting the people of Great

Britain against us, will raise such a storm against the measures of administration as will obstruct the war, and throw the kingdom into confusion.

A committee is appointed to prepare a confederation of the colonies, ascertaining the terms and ends of the compact and the limits of the Continental Constitution; and another committee is appointed to draw up a declaration that these colonies are free and independent states. And other committees are appointed for other purposes, as important. These committees will report in a week or two, and then the last finishing strokes will be given to the politics of this revolution. Nothing after that will remain but war. . . .[5]

John Adams Carries the Day

From his Autobiography.

Friday, June 28, 1776. A new delegation appeared from New Jersey. Mr. William Livingston and all others who had hitherto resisted independence were left out. Richard Stockton, Francis Hopkinson and Dr. John Witherspoon were new members.

Monday, July 1. A resolution of the Convention of Maryland, passed the 28th of June, was laid before Congress, and read, as follows:

That the instructions given to their deputies in December last be recalled, and the restriction therein contained, removed; and that their deputies to be authorized and empowered to concur with the other United Colonies, or a majority of them, in declaring the United Colonies free and independent states; in forming a compact between them, and in making foreign alliances, etc. . . .

I am not able to recollect whether it was on this or some preceding day that the greatest and most solemn debate was had on the question of independence. The subject had been in contemplation for more than a year, and frequent discussions had been had con-

77

cerning it. At one time and another all the arguments for it and against it had been exhausted and were become familiar. I expected no more would be said in public, but that the question would be put and decided. Mr. Dickinson, however, was determined to bear his testimony against it with more formality. He had prepared himself apparently with great labor and ardent zeal, and in a speech of great length, and with all his eloquence, he combined together all that had before been written in pamphlets and newspapers, and all that had from time to time been said in Congress by himself and others. He conducted the debate not only with great ingenuity and eloquence, but with equal politeness and candor, and was answered in the same spirit.

No member rose to answer him, and after waiting some time in hopes that some one less obnoxious than myself, who had been all along for a year before, and still was, represented and believed to be the author of all the mischief, would move, I determined to speak.

. . . I began by saying that this was the first time of my life that I had ever wished for the talents and eloquence of the ancient orators of Greece and Rome, for I was very sure that none of them ever had before him a question of more importance to his country and to the world. They would probably, upon less occasions than this, have begun by solemn invocations to their divinities for assistance; but the question before me appeared so simple that I had confidence enough in the plain understanding and common sense that had been given me to believe that I could answer, to the satisfaction of the House, all the arguments which had been produced, notwithstanding the abilities which had been displayed, and the eloquence with which they had been enforced.

Mr. Dickinson, some years afterward, published his speech. I had made no preparation beforehand and never committed any minutes of mine to writing. But if I had a copy of Mr. Dickinson's before me, I would now, after nine and twenty years have elapsed, endeavor to recollect mine.

Before the final question was put, the new delegates from New Jersey came in, and Mr. Stockton, Dr. Witherspoon and Mr. Hopkinson, very respectable characters, expressed a great desire to hear the arguments. All was silence; no one would speak; all eyes were turned upon me.

Mr. Edward Rutledge came to me and said, laughing, "Nobody will speak but you upon this subject. You have all the topics so ready that you must satisfy the gentlemen from New Jersey."

I answered him, laughing, that it had so much the air of exhibiting like an actor or gladiator, for the entertainment of the audience, that I was ashamed to repeat what I had said twenty times before, and I thought nothing new could be advanced by me. The New Jersey gentlemen, however, still insisting on hearing at least a recapitulation of the arguments, and no other gentleman being willing to speak, I summed up the reasons, objections and answers in as concise a manner as I could, till at length the Jersey gentlemen said they were fully satisfied and ready for the question, which was then put and determined in the affirmative.[6]

Caesar Rodney
in Boots and Spurs

Caesar Rodney in Boots and Spurs

Thomas McKean to Caesar A. Rodney.

Philadelphia, Sept. 22, 1813

Dear Sir . . . I recollect what passed in Congress in the beginning of July 1776, representing Independence. . . . On Monday the 1st of July the question was taken in the committee of the whole when the State of Pennsylvania (represented by seven gentlemen then present) voted against it. Delaware (having then only two representatives present) was divided; all the other states voted in favor of it. Whereupon, without delay, I sent an express (at my private expense) for your honored Uncle Caesar Rodney, Esquire, the remaining member for Delaware, whom I met at the Statehouse door, in his boots and spurs, as the members were assembling; after a little friendly salutation we went into the Hall of Congress together, and found we were among the latest; proceedings immediately commenced, and after a few minutes the great question was put; when the vote for Delaware was called, your uncle arose and said: "As I believe the voice of my constituents and of all sensible and honest men is in favor of Independence and my own judgment concurs with them, I vote for Independence" or in words to the same effect. . . .[7]

VII   THE GREAT DECLARATION

When, on June 10, Congress voted to postpone debate on Lee's resolution for independence for three weeks, it was foresighted enough to appoint a committee to draft a declaration of independence. This meant that if Congress *did* decide on independence, the declaration of causes would be all ready. To this committee the Congress named a representative group of five members from five different states: Thomas Jefferson from Virginia, Benjamin Franklin from Pennsylvania, John Adams from Massachusetts, Robert Livingston from New York, and Roger Sherman from Connecticut. For reasons still not wholly clear this committee in turn gave the job of writing the declaration to Thomas Jefferson.

It would not have been possible to make a better choice.

Just thirty-three years old at the time, Jefferson was one of the youngest members of the Congress, and one of the newest, but already well known. He had written an earlier statement of the American argument against the mother country—"A Summary View," it was called—and he had written, too, a large part of the "Declaration of the Causes and Necessity of Taking up Arms." Yet these papers, important as they were, gave no real indication of his abilities. Young as he was, he had two very remarkable qualities that fitted him almost perfectly for this particular task. First, he had a deep philosophical mind, a mind that grasped the issues and the arguments of the Revolutionary struggle, mastered them, marshaled them in battle array and sent them out to fight. And, second, he wrote like

81

an angel: no statesman in modern history has had a nobler literary style.

With the Declaration of Independence Thomas Jefferson was fairly launched on what was to be, all things considered, the most brilliant career in American history. There were still fifty years ahead of him (he—like John Adams—died on July 4, 1826!), and during the whole of those fifty years he served the nation whose birth certificate he had written. Member of Congress, co-author of the Virginia Constitution, author of the Virginia Statute for Religious Freedom, Governor of Virginia, author of the western Ordinances of 1784 and 1785, Minister to France, Secretary of State, Vice-President, twice President, responsible for the Louisiana Purchase and sponsor of the Monroe Doctrine—these were merely some of his public offices and contributions. In between he found time to run a big plantation; be a scientific farmer; invent a plow, a swivel chair, a writing machine and a dozen other gadgets; practice law and edit law books; collect the largest library in the country and found the Library of Congress; build the lovely house he called Monticello and design the beautiful buildings of the University of Virginia; play the violin; collect and study Indian languages; write the first natural history of Virginia; revise the penal code of Virginia; found the University of Virginia; translate the Greek dramatists; compile his own version of the Bible; draw up the rules of procedure for Congress; found and run the Democratic Party; write thousands of letters—all these and a few score other things as well.

But let us get back to the Declaration.

How was it written?

Considering what great letter writers Jefferson and Franklin and John Adams were, we know tantalizingly little about the actual drafting of the immortal document. There is no strictly contemporary account of the actual writing, and Jefferson—though he found time to write about almost everything else under the sun—never found time to give a really detailed and exact account of this central chapter of his life. And as for John Adams' recollections, these were written

Jefferson's Rough Draft of the Great Declaration

many years later, and at a time when Adams was jealous of Jefferson because he earned such fame by his authorship of the Declaration.

Yet it is possible to put together, from different sources, a pretty accurate account of what happened. We know, for example, that Jefferson wrote the Declaration in two weeks, for it was worked over by the committee and submitted to the Congress by June 28. We know that he wrote it standing up at his desk (still preserved) in the second-floor parlor of the house of a young German bricklayer named Graff. We know that in writing it he "turned neither to book nor pamphlet" but drew on his store of political philosophy and experience.

And we know, too, a good deal about the alterations by Franklin and Adams and other members of the committee, and then by the Congress. Most of these were just verbal changes—all to the good. But one of them was more than verbal. That was the omission of a thundering paragraph denouncing slavery and the slave trade, and blaming it all on George III! It was South Carolina and Georgia whose delegates objected to that paragraph: They were not ready for any criticism of slavery.

We know, too, that the Declaration, as it came from the hands of the committee, was debated on July 2, 3 and 4; that John Dickinson was the chief critic, and John Adams the chief defender—the "Atlas" of the debate, Jefferson later called him. Jefferson himself, apparently, sat silent through it all, preferring to have the document which he had written defended by others.

Whatever is still unclear about the drafting of the Declaration, one thing is clear beyond dispute: that the Declaration as we know it was the product of the mind and heart of Thomas Jefferson.

After almost three days of debate Congress adopted the Declaration "unanimously"—though New York still did not vote, and New York's representative on the committee, Robert Livingston, did not sign. A few days later, however, New York voted to accept the Declaration, so that made it really unanimous. There was a formal "signing" on August 2; a few men drifted in and signed later on that month; and eventually fifty-five Americans made themselves immortal by putting their names on the document. Thomas Jefferson's should have been the largest, but actually it was John Hancock of Massachusetts, who, as President of the Congress, signed with the biggest letters and in the most prominent place.

We give here five documents, or groups of documents. First comes Jefferson's own account of the making of the Declaration, written shortly after the event, but, alas, all too brief. Second are three accounts written almost half a century later, and therefore—because man's memory is faulty—not too trustworthy. The first of these is from the pungent pen of John Adams in reply to a letter from old

Timothy Pickering—a long-time enemy to Jefferson—who wanted to prove that Jefferson was not really very important in the writing of the Declaration! The second and third are from Jefferson's hand: one setting Adams and Pickering right on some details, the other explaining the broad philosophy of the Declaration. Third comes what is called Jefferson's "Rough Draft" of the Declaration—the Declaration as (in all probability) it was originally written by Jefferson and before the committee worked it over. It was in connection with the changes that the committee and members of Congress made in Jefferson's draft that wise old Benjamin Franklin told the story of John Thompson and his hats. We give here only the preamble—which you might compare with the preamble of the Declaration in its final form —and the paragraph on slavery that was struck out. Fourth is the Declaration itself, in its final and official form. And finally there is a group of letters and notes which tell something of the jubilation that greeted the Declaration of Independence.

"The Committee Desired Me to Draw the Declaration"

Jefferson's own account.

[Probably summer 1776]

It appearing in the course of these debates that the colonies of New York, New Jersey, Pennsylvania, Delaware, Maryland & South Carolina were not yet matured for falling from the parent stem, but that they were fast advancing to that state, it was thought most prudent to wait a while for them, and to postpone the final decisions to July 1, but that this might occasion as little delay as possible a committee was appointed to prepare a declaration of independence. the Commee. were J. Adams, Dr. Franklin, Roger Sherman, Robert R. Livingston & myself. committees were also appointed at the same time to prepare a plan of confederation for the colonies, and to state the terms proper to be proposed for foreign alliance.

the committee for drawing the declaration of Independence desired me to do it. it was accordingly done and being approved by them, I reported it to the house on Friday the 28th. of June when it was read and ordered to lie on the table.

on Monday the 1st. of July the house resolved itself into a commee. of the whole & resumed the consideration of the original motion made by the delegates of Virginia, which being again debated through the day, was carried in the affirmative by the votes of N. Hampshire, Connecticut, Massachusets, Rhode Island, N. Jersey, Maryland, Virginia, N. Carolina, & Georgia. S. Carolina and Pennsylvania voted against it. Delaware having but two members present, they were divided: the delegates for New York declared they were for it themselves, & were assured their constituents were for it, but that their instructions having been drawn near a twelvemonth before, when reconciliation was still the general object, they were enjoined by them to do nothing which should impede that object. they therefore thought themselves not justifiable in voting on either side, and asked leave to withdraw from the question, which was given them.

the Commee. rose & reported their resolution to the house. Mr. Rutledge of S. Carolina then requested the determination might be put off to the next day, as he believed his collegues, tho' they disapproved of the resolution, would then join in it for the sake of unanimity. the ultimate question whether the house would agree to the resolution of the committee was accordingly postponed to the next day [July 2], when it was again moved and S. Carolina concurred in voting for it. in the mean time a third member had come post from the Delaware counties and turned the vote of that colony in favor of the resolution. members of a different sentiment attending that morning from Pennsylvania also, their vote was changed, so that the whole 12 colonies who were authorized to vote at all, gave their voices for it: and within a few days the convention of N. York approved of it and thus supplied the void occasioned by the withdrawing of their delegates from the vote.

Signing the Declaration

Congress proceeded the same day [July 2] to consider the declaration of Independence, which had been reported & laid on the table the Friday preceding, and on Monday referred to a commee. of the whole. the pusillanimous idea that we had friends in England worth keeping terms with, still haunted the minds of many. for this reason those passages which conveyed censures on the people of England were struck out, lest they should give them offense. the clause too, reprobating the enslaving the inhabitants of Africa, was struck out in complaisance to South Carolina & Georgia, who had never attempted to restrain the importation of slaves and who on the contrary still wished to continue it. our Northern brethren also I believe felt a little tender under those censures; for tho' their people have very few slaves themselves yet they had been pretty considerable carriers of them to others. The debates having taken up the greater parts of the 2d. 3d. & 4th. days of July were, in the evening of the last closed. the declaration was reported by the commee., agreed to by the house, and signed by every member present except Mr. Dickinson.[1]

John Adams Places Virginia at the Head of Everything

To Timothy Pickering.

August 6, 1822

You inquire why so young a man as Mr. Jefferson was placed at the head of the committee for preparing a Declaration of Independence? I answer: It was the Frankfort advice to place Virginia at the head of everything. Mr. Richard Henry Lee might be gone to Virginia, to his sick family, for aught I know, but that was not the reason for Mr. Jefferson's appointment. There were three committees appointed at the same time, one for the Declaration of Independence, another for preparing articles of confederation, and another for preparing a treaty to be proposed to France. Mr. Lee was chosen for the Committee of Confederation, and it was not thought convenient that the same person should be upon both.

Mr. Jefferson came into Congress in June, 1775, and brought with him a reputation for literature, science, and a happy talent of composition. Writings of his were handed about, remarkable for the peculiar felicity of expression. Though a silent member in Congress, he was so prompt, frank, explicit and decisive upon committees and in conversation—not even Samuel Adams was more so—that he soon seized upon my heart; and upon this occasion I gave him my vote, and did all in my power to procure the votes of others. I think he had one more vote than any other, and that placed him at the head of the committee. I had the next highest number, and that placed me the second. The committee met, discussed the subject, and then appointed Mr. Jefferson and me to make the draft, I suppose because we were the two first on the list.

The subcommittee met. Jefferson proposed to me to make the draft.

I said, "I will not."

"You should do it."

"Oh! no."

"Why will you not? You ought to do it."

"I will not."

"Why?"

"Reason enough."

"What can be your reasons?"

"Reason first—You are a Virginian, and a Virginian ought to appear at the head of this business. Reason second—I am obnoxious, suspected and unpopular. You are very much otherwise. Reason third—You can write ten times better than I can."

"Well," said Jefferson, "if you are decided, I will do as well as I can."

"Very well. When you have drawn it up, we will have a meeting."

A meeting we accordingly had, and conned the paper over. I was delighted with its high tone and the flights of oratory with which it abounded. . . . There were other expressions which I would not have inserted, if I had drawn it up, particularly that which called the King tyrant. I thought this too personal; for I never believed George to be a tyrant in disposition and in nature; I always believed him to be deceived by his courtiers on both sides of the Atlantic, and, in his official capacity only, cruel. I thought the expression too passionate, and too much like scolding, for so grave and solemn a document; but as Franklin and Sherman were to inspect it afterwards, I thought it would not become me to strike it out. I consented to report it, and do not now remember that I made or suggested a single alteration.

We reported it to the committee of five. It was read, and I do

not remember that Franklin or Sherman criticized any thing.
We were all in haste. Congress was impatient, and the instrument
was reported, as I believe, in Jefferson's handwriting, as he first
drew it. Congress cut off about a quarter of it, as I expected they
would; but they obliterated some of the best of it, and left all that
was exceptionable, if any thing in it was. I have long wondered
that the original draft has not been published. I suppose the
reason is the vehement philippic against Negro slavery.

As you justly observe, there is not an idea in it but what had
been hackneyed in Congress for two years before. The substance
of it is contained in the declaration of rights and the violation of
those rights, in the Journals of Congress, in 1774. Indeed, the
essence of it is contained in a pamphlet, voted and printed by
the town of Boston, before the first Congress met, composed by
James Otis, as I suppose, in one of his lucid intervals, and pruned
and polished by Samuel Adams.[2]

"I Turned to Neither Book nor Pamphlet"

Thomas Jefferson to James Madison.

Monticello, August 30, 1823

Dear Sir, . . . The committee of five met; no such thing as a
sub-committee was proposed, but they unanimously pressed on
myself alone to undertake the draught. I consented; I drew it; but
before I reported it to the committee, I communicated it *separately*
to Dr. Franklin and Mr. Adams, requesting their corrections, because they were the two members of whose judgments and amendments I wished most to have the benefit before presenting it to
the committee. . . . Their alterations were two or three only, and
merely verbal. I then wrote a fair copy, reported it to the committee, and from them, unaltered, to Congress. This personal com-
munication and consultation with Mr. Adams, he has misremem-
bered into the actings of a sub-committee.

Pickering's observations, and Mr. Adams' in addition, "that it contained no new ideas, that it is a common-place compilation, its sentiments hacknied in Congress for two years before, and its essence contained in Otis's pamphlet" may all be true. Of that I am not to be the judge. Richard Henry Lee charged it as copied from Locke's treatise on government. Otis' pamphlet I never saw and whether I had gathered my ideas from reading or reflection I do not know. I only know that I turned to neither book nor pamphlet while writing it. I did not consider it as any part of my charge to invent new ideas altogether, and to offer no sentiment which had ever been expressed before. Had Mr. Adams been so restrained, Congress would have lost the benefit of his bold and impressive advocations of the rights of Revolution. For no man's confident and fervid addresses, more than Mr. Adams', encouraged and supported us through the difficulties surrounding us, which, like the ceaseless action of gravity weighed on us by night and by day. Yet on the same ground, we may ask what of these elevated thoughts was new, or can be affirmed never before to have entered the conceptions of man?

Whether, also, the sentiments of Independence, and the reasons for declaring it, which make so great a portion of the instrument, had been hackneyed in Congress for two years before the 4th of July '76, or this dictum also of Mr. Adams be another slip of memory, let history say. This, however, I will say for Mr. Adams, that he supported the Declaration with zeal and ability, fighting fearlessly for every word of it. As to myself, I thought it a duty to be, on that occasion, a passive auditor of the opinions of others, more impartial judges than I could be, of its merits or demerits. During the debate I was sitting by Doctor Franklin, and he observed that I was writhing a little under the acrimonious criticisms of some of its parts; and it was on that occasion, that by way of comfort, he told me the story of John Thompson, the hatter, and his new sign.[3]

Here is the story that Franklin told Jefferson:

91

"I have made it a rule," said he, "whenever in my power, to avoid becoming the draftsman of papers to be reviewed by a public body. I took my lesson from an incident which I will relate to you.

"When I was a journeyman printer one of my companions, an apprentice hatter, having served out his time was about to open shop for himself. His first concern was to have a handsome signboard with a proper inscription. He composed it in these words: 'John Thompson, hatter, makes and sells hats for ready money,' with a figure of a hat subjoined. But he thought he would submit it to his friends for their amendments.

"The first he showed it to thought the word 'hatter' tautologous, because followed by the words 'makes hats' which show he was a hatter. It was struck out.

"The next observed that the word 'makes' might as well be omitted, because the customers would not care who made the hats. If good and to their mind, they would buy, by whomever made. He struck it out.

"A third said he thought the words 'for ready money' were useless, as it was not the custom of the place to sell on credit. Everyone who purchased expected to pay. They were parted with, and the inscription now stood: 'John Thompson sells hats.'

" 'Sells hats?' " says his next friend. 'Why, nobody will expect you to give them away. What then is the use of that word?' It was stricken out; and 'hats' followed it, the rather as there was one painted on the board.

"So his inscription was reduced ultimately to 'John Thompson' with the figure of a hat subjoined."[4]

"It Was Intended to Be an Expression of the American Mind"

Thomas Jefferson to Henry Lee.

Monticello, May 8, 1825

... With respect to our rights, and the acts of the British government contravening those rights, there was but one opinion on this side of the water. All American whigs thought alike on these subjects. When forced, therefore, to resort to arms for redress, an appeal to the tribunal of the world was deemed proper for our justification. This was the object of the Declaration of Independence. Not to find out new principles, or new arguments, never before thought of, not merely to say things which had never been said before; but to place before mankind the common sense of the subject, in terms so plain and firm as to command their assent, and to justify ourselves in the independent stand we are compelled to take. Neither aiming at originality of principle or sentiment, nor yet copied from any particular and previous writing, it was intended to be an expression of the American mind, and to give to that expression the proper tone and spirit called for by the occasion. All its authority rests then on the harmonizing sentiments of the day, whether expressed in conversation, in letters, printed essays, or in the elementary books of public right, as Aristotle, Cicero, Locke, Sidney, etc. . . .[5]

Jefferson's Rough Draft of the Declaration

A Declaration of the Representatives of the United States of America, in General Congress assembled.

When in the course of human events it becomes necessary for a people to advance from that subordination in which they have hitherto remained, and to assume among the powers of the earth the equal and independant station to which the laws of nature and of nature's god entitle them, a decent respect to the opinions of mankind requires that they should declare the causes which impel them to the change.

We hold these truths to be sacred and undeniable; that all men are created equal and independant, that from that equal creation they derive rights inherent and inalienable, among which are the preservation of life, and liberty and the pursuit of happiness; that to secure these ends, governments are instituted among men,

93

deriving their just powers from the consent of the governed; that whenever any form of government shall become destructive of these ends, it is the right of the people to alter or to abolish it, and to institute new government, laying it's foundation on such principles and organising its powers in such form, as to them shall seem most likely to effect their safety and happiness. prudence indeed will dictate that government long established should not be changed for light and transient causes: and accordingly all experience hath shewn that mankind are more disposed to suffer while evils are sufferable, than to right themselves by abolishing the forms to which they are accustomed. but when a long train of abuses and usurpations, begun at a distinguished period, and pursuing invariably the same object, evinces a design to subject them to arbitrary power, it is their right, it is their duty, to throw off such government and to provide new guards for their future security. such has been the patient sufferance of these colonies; and such is now the necessity which constrains them to expunge their former systems of government. the history of his present majesty, is a history of unremitting injuries and usurpations, among which no one fact stands single or solitary to contradict the uniform tenor of the rest, all of which have in direct object the establishment of an absolute tyranny over these states. to prove this, let facts be submitted to a candid world, for the truth of which we pledge a faith yet unsullied by falsehood. . . .

The Clause Against Slavery

. . . he has waged cruel war against human nature itself, violating it's most sacred rights of life & liberty in the persons of a distant people who never offended him, captivating & carrying them into slavery in another hemisphere, or to incur miserable death in their transportation thither. This piratical warfare, the opprobrium of *infidel* powers, is the warfare of the CHRISTIAN king of Great Britain, determined to keep open a market where

MEN should be bought and sold, he has prostituted his negative for suppressing every legislative attempt to prohibit or to restrain this execrable commerce: and that this assemblage of horrors might want no fact of distinguished die, he is now exciting those very people to rise in arms among us, and to purchase that liberty of which *he* has deprived them, by murdering the people upon whom he also obtruded them; thus paying off former crimes committed against the *liberties* of one people, with crimes which he urges them to commit against the *lives* of another.[6]

THE DECLARATION OF INDEPENDENCE

In Congress, July 4, 1776
The Unanimous Declaration of the Thirteen
United States of America

When in the Course of human events, it becomes necessary for one people to dissolve the political bands which have connected them with another, and to assume among the Powers of the earth, the separate and equal station to which the Laws of Nature and of Nature's God entitle them, a decent respect to the opinions of mankind requires that they should declare the causes which impel them to the separation.

We hold these truths to be self-evident, that all men are created equal, that they are endowed by their Creator with certain unalienable Rights, that among these are Life, Liberty and the pursuit of Happiness. That to secure these rights, Governments are instituted among Men, deriving their just powers from the consent of the governed, That whenever any Form of Government becomes destructive of these ends, it is the Right of the People to alter or to abolish it, and to institute new Government, laying its foundation on such principles and organizing its powers in such form, as to them shall seem most likely to effect their Safety and Happiness. Prudence, indeed, will dictate that Governments long established should not be changed for light and transient causes; and accordingly all experience hath shown, that mankind are more disposed to suffer, while evils are sufferable, than to right themselves by abolishing the forms to which they are accustomed. But when a long train of abuses and usurpations, pursuing invariably the same Object evinces a design to reduce them under absolute Despotism, it is their right, it is their duty, to throw off such Government, and to provide new Guards for their future security.—Such has been the patient sufferance of these Colonies; and such is now the necessity which constrains them to alter their former Systems of Government. The history of the present King of Great Britain is a history of repeated injuries and usurpations, all having in direct object the establishment of an absolute Tyranny over these States. To prove this, let Facts be submitted to a candid world.

He has refused his Assent to Laws, the most wholesome and necessary for the public good.

He has forbidden his Governors to pass Laws of immediate and pressing importance, unless suspended in their operation till his Assent should be obtained; and when so suspended, he has utterly neglected to attend to them.

He has refused to pass other Laws for the accommodation of large districts of people, unless those people would relinquish the right of Representation in the Legislature, a right inestimable to them and formidable to tyrants only.

He has called together legislative bodies at places unusual, uncomfortable, and distant from the depository of their Public Records, for the sole purpose of fatiguing them into compliance with his measures.

He has dissolved Representative Houses repeatedly, for opposing with manly firmness his invasions on the rights of the people.

He has refused for a long time, after such dissolutions, to cause others to be elected; whereby the Legislative Powers, incapable of Annihilation, have returned to the People at large for their exercise; the State remaining in the mean time exposed to all the dangers of invasion from without, and convulsions within.

He has endeavoured to prevent the population of these States; for that purpose obstructing the Laws of Naturalization of Foreigners; refusing to pass others to encourage their migration hither, and raising the conditions of new Appropriations of Lands.

He has obstructed the Administration of Justice, by refusing his Assent to Laws for establishing Judiciary Powers.

He has made Judges dependent on his Will alone, for the tenure of their offices, and the amount and payment of their salaries.

He has erected a multitude of New Offices, and sent hither swarms of Officers to harass our People, and eat out their substance.

He has kept among us, in times of peace, Standing Armies without the Consent of our legislature.

He has affected to render the Military independent of and superior to the Civil Power.

He has combined with others to subject us to a jurisdiction foreign to our constitution, and unacknowledged by our laws; giving his Assent to their acts of pretended legislation:

For quartering large bodies of armed troops among us:

For protecting them, by a mock Trial, from Punishment for any Murders which they should commit on the Inhabitants of these States:

For cutting off our Trade with all parts of the world:

For imposing taxes on us without our Consent:

For depriving us in many cases, of the benefits of Trial by Jury:

For transporting us beyond Seas to be tried for pretended offences:

For abolishing the free System of English Laws in a neighbouring Province, establishing therein an Arbitrary government, and enlarging its Boundaries so as to render it at once an example and fit instrument for introducing the same absolute rule into these Colonies:

For taking away our Charters, abolishing our most valuable Laws, and altering fundamentally the Forms of our Governments.

For suspending our own Legislature, and declaring themselves invested with Power to legislate for us in all cases whatsoever.

He has abdicated Government here, by declaring us out of his Protection and waging War against us.

He has plundered our seas, ravaged our Coasts, burnt our towns, and destroyed the lives of our people.

He is at this time transporting large armies of foreign mercenaries to compleat the works of death, desolation and tyranny, already begun with circumstances of Cruelty & perfidy scarcely paralleled in the most barbarous ages, and totally unworthy the Head of a civilized nation.

He has constrained our fellow Citizens taken Captive on the high Seas to bear Arms against their Country, to become the executioners of their friends and Brethren, or to fall themselves by their Hands.

He has excited domestic insurrections amongst us, and has endeavoured to bring on the inhabitants of our frontiers, the merciless Indian Savages, whose known rule of warfare, is an undistinguished destruction of all ages, sexes and conditions.

In every stage of these Oppressions We have Petitioned for Redress in the most humble terms: Our repeated Petitions have been answered only by repeated injury. A Prince, whose character is thus marked by every act which may define a Tyrant, is unfit to be the ruler of a free People.

Nor have We been wanting in attention to our Brittish brethren. We have warned them from time to time of attempts by their legislature to extend an unwarrantable jurisdiction over us. We have reminded them of the circumstances of our emigration and settlement here. We have appealed to their native justice and magnanimity, and we have conjured them by the ties of our common kindred to disavow these usurpations, which would inevitably interrupt our connections and correspondence. They too have been deaf to the voice of justice and of consanguinity. We must, therefore, acquiesce in the necessity, which denounces our Separation, and hold them, as we hold the rest of mankind, Enemies in War, in Peace Friends.

We, therefore, the Representatives of the united States of America, in General Congress, Assembled, appealing to the Supreme Judge of the world for the rectitude of our intentions, do, in the Name and by Authority of the good People of these Colonies, solemnly publish and declare, That these United Colonies are, and of Right ought to be Free and Independent States; that they are Absolved from all Allegiance to the British Crown, and that all political connection between them and the State of Great Britain, is and ought to be totally dissolved; and that as Free and Independent States, they have full Power to levy War, conclude Peace, contract Alliances, establish Commerce, and to do all other Acts and Things which Independent States may of right do. And for the support of this Declaration, with a firm reliance on the Protection of Divine Providence, we mutually pledge to each other our Lives, our Fortunes and our sacred Honor.[7]

JOHN HANCOCK

New Hampshire
 JOSIAH BARTLETT,
 WM. WHIPPLE,
 MATTHEW THORNTON.

Massachusetts-Bay
 SAML. ADAMS,
 JOHN ADAMS,
 ROBT. TREAT PAINE,
 ELBRIDGE GERRY.

New York
 WM. FLOYD,
 PHIL. LIVINGSTON,
 FRANS. LEWIS,
 LEWIS MORRIS.

Rhode Island
 STEP. HOPKINS,
 WILLIAM ELLERY.

Connecticut
ROGER SHERMAN,
SAM'EL HUNTINGTON,
WM. WILLIAMS,
OLIVER WOLCOTT.

Georgia
BUTTON GWINNETT,
LYMAN HALL,
GEO. WALTON.

Maryland
SAMUEL CHASE,
WM. PACA,
THOS. STONE,
CHARLES CARROLL
   of Carrollton.

Virginia
GEORGE WYTHE,
RICHARD HENRY LEE,
TH. JEFFERSON,
BENJA. HARRISON,
THS. NELSON, JR.,
FRANCIS LIGHTFOOT LEE,
CARTER BRAXTON.

Pennsylvania
ROBT. MORRIS,
BENJAMIN RUSH,
BENJA. FRANKLIN,
JOHN MORTON,
GEO. CLYMER,
JAS. SMITH,
GEO. TAYLOR,
JAMES WILSON,
GEO. ROSS.

Delaware
CAESAR RODNEY,
GEO. READ,
THO. M'KEAN.

North Carolina
WM. HOOPER,
JOSEPH HEWES,
JOHN PENN.

South Carolina
EDWARD RUTLEDGE,
THOS. HEYWARD, JUNR.,
THOMAS LYNCH, JUNR.,
ARTHUR MIDDLETON.

New Jersey
RICHD. STOCKTON,
JNO. WITHERSPOON,
FRAS. HOPKINSON,
JOHN HART,
ABRA. CLARK.

IN CONGRESS, JULY 4, 1776.

The unanimous Declaration of the thirteen united States of America.

When in the Course of human events, it becomes necessary for one people to dissolve the political bands which have connected them with another, and to assume among the powers of the earth, the separate and equal station to which the Laws of Nature and of Nature's God entitle them, a decent respect to the opinions of mankind requires that they should declare the causes which impel them to the separation. — We hold these truths to be self-evident, that all men are created equal, that they are endowed by their Creator with certain unalienable Rights, that among these are Life, Liberty and the pursuit of Happiness. — That to secure these rights, Governments are instituted among Men, deriving their just powers from the consent of the governed, — That whenever any Form of Government becomes destructive of these ends, it is the Right of the People to alter or to abolish it, and to institute new Government, laying its foundation on such principles and organizing its powers in such form, as to them shall seem most likely to effect their Safety and Happiness. Prudence, indeed, will dictate that Governments long established should not be changed for light and transient causes; and accordingly all experience hath shewn, that mankind are more disposed to suffer, while evils are sufferable, than to right themselves by abolishing the forms to which they are accustomed. But when a long train of abuses and usurpations, pursuing invariably the same Object evinces a design to reduce them under absolute Despotism, it is their right, it is their duty, to throw off such Government, and to provide new Guards for their future security. — Such is now the patient sufferance of these Colonies; and such is now the necessity which constrains them to alter their former Systems of Government. The history of the present King of Great Britain is a history of repeated injuries and usurpations, all having in direct object the establishment of an absolute Tyranny over these States. To prove this, let Facts be submitted to a candid world.

He has refused his Assent to Laws, the most wholesome and necessary for the public good. — He has forbidden his Governors to pass Laws of immediate and pressing importance, unless suspended in their operation till his Assent should be obtained; and when so suspended, he has utterly neglected to attend to them. — He has refused to pass other Laws for the accommodation of large districts of people, unless those people would relinquish the right of Representation in the Legislature, a right inestimable to them and formidable to tyrants only. — He has called together legislative bodies at places unusual, uncomfortable, and distant from the depository of their public Records, for the sole purpose of fatiguing them into compliance with his measures. — He has dissolved Representative Houses repeatedly, for opposing with manly firmness his invasions on the rights of the people. — He has refused for a long time, after such dissolutions, to cause others to be elected; whereby the Legislative powers, incapable of Annihilation, have returned to the People at large for their exercise; the State remaining in the mean time exposed to all the dangers of invasion from without, and convulsions within. — He has endeavoured to prevent the population of these States; for that purpose obstructing the Laws for Naturalization of Foreigners; refusing to pass others to encourage their migrations hither, and raising the conditions of new Appropriations of Lands. — He has obstructed the Administration of Justice, by refusing his Assent to Laws for establishing Judiciary powers. — He has made Judges dependent on his Will alone, for the tenure of their offices, and the amount and payment of their salaries. — He has erected a multitude of New Offices, and sent hither swarms of Officers to harrass our people, and eat out their substance. — He has kept among us, in times of peace, Standing Armies without the Consent of our legislatures. — He has affected to render the Military independent of and superior to the Civil power. — He has combined with others to subject us to a jurisdiction foreign to our constitution, and unacknowledged by our laws; giving his Assent to their Acts of pretended Legislation: — For quartering large bodies of armed troops among us: — For protecting them, by a mock Trial, from punishment for any Murders which they should commit on the Inhabitants of these States: — For cutting off our Trade with all parts of the world: — For imposing Taxes on us without our Consent: — For depriving us in many cases, of the benefits of Trial by Jury: — For transporting us beyond Seas to be tried for pretended offences: — For abolishing the free System of English Laws in a neighbouring Province, establishing therein an Arbitrary government, and enlarging its Boundaries so as to render it at once an example and fit instrument for introducing the same absolute rule into these Colonies: — For taking away our Charters, abolishing our most valuable Laws, and altering fundamentally the Forms of our Governments: — For suspending our own Legislatures, and declaring themselves invested with power to legislate for us in all cases whatsoever. — He has abdicated Government here, by declaring us out of his Protection and waging War against us. — He has plundered our seas, ravaged our Coasts, burnt our towns, and destroyed the lives of our people. — He is at this time transporting large Armies of foreign Mercenaries to compleat the works of death, desolation and tyranny, already begun with circumstances of Cruelty & perfidy scarcely paralleled in the most barbarous ages, and totally unworthy the Head of a civilized nation. — He has constrained our fellow Citizens taken Captive on the high Seas to bear Arms against their Country, to become the executioners of their friends and Brethren, or to fall themselves by their Hands. — He has excited domestic insurrections amongst us, and has endeavoured to bring on the inhabitants of our frontiers, the merciless Indian Savages, whose known rule of warfare, is an undistinguished destruction of all ages, sexes and conditions. In every stage of these Oppressions We have Petitioned for Redress in the most humble terms: Our repeated Petitions have been answered only by repeated injury. A Prince, whose character is thus marked by every act which may define a Tyrant, is unfit to be the ruler of a free people. Nor have We been wanting in attentions to our British brethren. We have warned them from time to time of attempts by their legislature to extend an unwarrantable jurisdiction over us. We have reminded them of the circumstances of our emigration and settlement here. We have appealed to their native justice and magnanimity, and we have conjured them by the ties of our common kindred to disavow these usurpations, which would inevitably interrupt our connections and correspondence. They too have been deaf to the voice of justice and of consanguinity. We must, therefore, acquiesce in the necessity, which denounces our Separation, and hold them, as we hold the rest of mankind, Enemies in War, in Peace Friends. —

We, therefore, the Representatives of the united States of America, in General Congress, Assembled, appealing to the Supreme Judge of the world for the rectitude of our intentions, do, in the Name, and by Authority of the good People of these Colonies, solemnly publish and declare, That these United Colonies are, and of Right ought to be Free and Independent States; that they are Absolved from all Allegiance to the British Crown, and that all political connection between them and the State of Great Britain, is and ought to be totally dissolved; and that as Free and Independent States, they have full Power to levy War, conclude Peace, contract Alliances, establish Commerce, and to do all other Acts and Things which Independent States may of right do. — And for the support of this Declaration, with a firm reliance on the protection of divine Providence, we mutually pledge to each other our Lives, our Fortunes and our sacred Honor.

Button Gwinnett
Lyman Hall
Geo Walton.

Wm Hooper
Joseph Hewes,
John Penn

Edward Rutledge.
Thos Heyward Junr.
Thomas Lynch Junr.
Arthur Middleton

John Hancock

Samuel Chase
Wm Paca
Thos Stone
Charles Carroll of Carrollton

George Wythe
Richard Henry Lee
Th Jefferson
Benja Harrison
Thos Nelson jr.
Francis Lightfoot Lee
Carter Braxton

Robt Morris
Benjamin Rush
Benja Franklin
John Morton
Geo Clymer
Jas Smith.
Geo Taylor
James Wilson
Geo. Ross
Caesar Rodney
Geo Read
Tho M:Kean

Wm Floyd
Phil. Livingston
Frans Lewis
Lewis Morris

Richd Stockton
Jno Witherspoon
Fras Hopkinson
John Hart
Abra Clark

Josiah Bartlett
Wm Whipple
Saml Adams
John Adams
Robt Treat Paine
Elbridge Gerry
Step Hopkins
William Ellery
Roger Sherman
Samel Huntington
Wm Williams
Oliver Wolcott
Matthew Thornton

"A Greater Question Never Will Be Decided among Men"

John Adams to Abigail Adams.

Philadelphia, 3 July, 1776

... Yesterday the greatest question was decided which ever was debated in America, and a greater, perhaps, never was nor will be decided among men. A resolution was passed without one dissenting colony, "that these United Colonies are, and of right ought to be, free and independent States, and as such they have, and of right ought to have, full power to make war, conclude peace, establish commerce, and to do all other acts and things which other States may rightfully do." You will see in a few days a Declaration setting forth the causes which have impelled us to this mighty revolution, and the reasons which will justify it in the sight of God and man. A plan of confederation will be taken up in a few days.

When I look back to the year 1761, and recollect the argument concerning writs of assistance in the superior court, which I have hitherto considered as the commencement of this controversy between Great Britain and America, and run through the whole period from that time to this, and recollect the series of political events, the chain of causes and effects, I am surprised at the suddenness as well as greatness of this revolution. Britain has been filled with folly, and America with wisdom. At least, this is my judgment. Time must determine. It is the will of Heaven that the two countries should be sundered forever. It may be the will of Heaven that America shall suffer calamities still more wasting, and distress yet more dreadful. If this is to be the case, it will have this good effect at least. It will inspire us with many virtues which we have not, and correct many errors, follies and vices which threaten to disturb, dishonor and destroy us. The furnace of affliction produces refinement, in States as well as individuals. And the new governments we are assuming in every part will require a purification from our vices, and an augmentation of our

102

virtues, or they will be no blessings. The people will have un-
bounded power, and the people are extremely addicted to corruption and venality, as well as the great. But I must submit all my
hopes and fears to an overruling Providence, in which, unfashion-
able as the faith may be, I firmly believe.[8]

"Rays of Ravishing Light and Glory"

John Adams to Abigail Adams.

July 3, 1776

The second day of July, 1776, will be the most memorable
epocha in the history of America. I am apt to believe that it will
be celebrated by succeeding generations as the great anniversary
festival. It ought to be commemorated as the day of deliverance,
by solemn acts of devotion to God Almighty. It ought to be solemn-
ized with pomp and parade, with shows, games, sports, guns, bells,
bonfires and illuminations, from one end of this continent to the
other, from this time forward, forevermore.

You will think me transported with enthusiasm, but I am not.
I am well aware of the toil, and blood, and treasure that it will
cost us to maintain this declaration, and support and defend these
states. Yet, through all the gloom, I can see the rays of ravishing
light and glory. I can see that the end is more than worth all the
means, and that posterity will triumph in that day's transaction,
even although we should rue it, which I trust in God we shall not.[9]

"The Bells Rang All Day and Almost All Night"

John Adams to Samuel Chase.

Philadelphia, July 9, 1776

Yours of the 5th came to me the 8th. You will see by this post
that the river is passed, and the bridge cut away. The Declaration
was yesterday published and proclaimed from that awful stage in
the State-house yard; by whom, do you think? By the Committee

103

The Colonies Declare Themselves Independent

of Safety, the Committee of Inspection, and a great crowd of
people. Three cheers rended the welkin. The battalions paraded
on the Common, and gave us the *feu de joie*, notwithstanding the
scarcity of powder. The bells rang all day and almost all night.
Even the chimers chimed away. . . .

As soon as an American seal is prepared, I conjecture the Declarations will be subscribed by all the members, which will give you the opportunity you wish for, of transmitting your name among the votaries of independence.[10]

"The Thirteen United Colonies"

From the Diary of Ezra Stiles.

July 13, 1776. Mr. Channing returned from Newport and brought the Congresses Declaration of INDEPENDENCY dated at Philadelphia the fourth day of July instant. This I read at noon, and for the first time realized Independency. Thus the CONGRESS have tied a Gordian knot, which the Parliament will find they can neither cut nor untie. The *thirteen united Colonies* now rise into an *Independent Republic* among the kingdoms, states and empires on earth. May the Supreme and Omnipotent Lord of the Monarchical Republic of the immense Universe shower down his blessings upon it, and ever keep it under his holy protection.[11]

Something, finally, must be said about the Declaration itself. It is one of those things, like "The Star Spangled Banner," that everybody thinks he knows by heart but that few people actually do know by heart. You probably took for granted that you know it, and skipped over it instead of reading it. But it is worth careful reading.

There are two main parts to the Declaration. First comes the philosophical argument: Americans have certain fundamental rights; the King has violated these rights, and has thereby confessed that his purpose is to establish a tyranny over the American people. The second part contains the evidence to support this argument—"facts submitted to a candid world." It consists of a long series of examples of tyranny by George III.

This "long train of abuses and usurpations" (twenty-seven of them altogether) need not detain us very long. Note, first, that they are all blamed on poor George III. That is not because George III was such a wicked man; actually he was a stupid but well-meaning King. It is because the Americans took the position that Parliament had no authority over them whatsoever. Therefore every act to which they objected had to be an act of the King!

Most of the charges are based on fact, but the facts themselves are in many instances matters of dispute. Some of them, for example, refer to what happened *after* Lexington and Concord: the Americans were saying, in effect, that to put down a rebellion is itself an act of tyranny, and therefore justifies the rebellion! Others misrepresent the purposes of British laws: thus, for example, the one about "abolishing the free system of Laws in a neighboring province." That referred to the Quebec Act of 1774—in reality a very progressive piece of legislation which tried to provide the French Canadians with their own system of laws instead of the alien English system.

But these comments are in a sense beside the point. The point is that Jefferson was not writing history; he was making a revolution.

Far more important is the first section of the Declaration—the philosophical argument. Here Jefferson set forth with masterly skill a series of "self-evident truths." What are these truths?

There are, altogether, seven of them:

1. That all men are created equal.
2. That all men have inborn rights that cannot be taken away from them.
3. That among these rights are life, liberty and happiness—or the "pursuit" of happiness.
4. That the primary purpose of government is to preserve these rights.
5. That government gets all its powers from the consent of the governed.
6. That if government fails to protect men in their rights, men have the right and the duty to change it or to abolish it altogether.
7. That they have the right, then, to create new governments—governments that will, in fact, provide them with safety and happiness.

Now the first thing we note about these principles, or doctrines, is that they seem to us, as they seemed to Jefferson, the common sense of the matter. We haven't found them too hard to understand, and we haven't outgrown them. The reason is, of course, that these arguments are not just passing thoughts, useful for the moment, but permanent principles, as valid today as yesterday, and as valid tomorrow as today. The second thing we note is that these principles do in fact refer to "all men," not just to Americans. They are America's birthright, but they're also man's birthright. They have spread from America throughout the whole civilized world.

The Declaration of Independence belongs to world history, and is the possession of all mankind.

"Proclaim Liberty throughout all the Land to all the Inhabitants thereof." Lev. xxv:10.
—Inscription on the Liberty Bell

ACKNOWLEDGMENTS *(Continued)*

H.S.C.

NOTES

Chapter I

1. Charles Francis Adams (ed.), *The Works of John Adams* (Boston, 1850-1856), IX, 420.

Chapter II

1. George W. Corner (ed.), *The Autobiography of Benjamin Rush* (Princeton University Press for the American Philosophical Society, 1948), pp. 139-158 *passim*.

Chapter III

1. Worthington Chauncey Ford (ed.), *Journals of the Continental Congress* (Washington: Library of Congress, 1904-1937), II, 140ff.
2. Peter Force (ed.), *American Archives* (Washington, 1837-1853), 4th Series, II, 1870-1871.
3. Adams (ed.), *The Works of John Adams*, II, 410-411.
4. Adams (ed.), *The Works of John Adams*, II, 411n.
5. Force (ed.), *American Archives*, 4th Series, III, 240-241.

Chapter IV

1. Force (ed.), *American Archives*, 4th Series, III, 1706-1707.
2. Force (ed.), *American Archives*, 4th Series, IV, 572.
3. Corner (ed.), *The Autobiography of Benjamin Rush*, pp. 113-114.
4. Thomas Paine, *Common Sense, passim*.

Chapter V

1. *Warren-Adams Letters* (Boston: Massachusetts Historical Society, 1917-1925), I, 224-225.
2. James Austin, *The Life of Elbridge Gerry*, pp. 175-176.
3. *Warren-Adams Letters*, I, 249.
4. *Warren-Adams Letters*, I, 249-251.
5. Massachusetts Archives, CLVI, 103.

6. Massachusetts Archives, CLVI, 103.

7. Force (ed.), *American Archives*, 4th Series, VI, 829.

8. Julian P. Boyd (ed.), *Papers of Thomas Jefferson* (Princeton, 1950-1955), I, 290-291.

9. Force (ed.), *American Archives*, 4th Series, VI, 466.

Chapter VI

1. Ford (ed.), *Journals of the Continental Congress*, V, 425.

2. Boyd (ed.), *Papers of Thomas Jefferson*, I, 309-313.

3. Adams (ed.), *The Works of John Adams*, IX, 387-388.

4. Adams (ed.), *The Works of John Adams*, IX, 391.

5. Adams (ed.), *The Works of John Adams*, IX, 409-410.

6. Adams (ed.), *The Works of John Adams*, III, 53-58.

7. Burnett (ed.), *Letters of Members of the Continental Congress*, I, 760.

Chapter VII

1. Boyd (ed.), *Papers of Thomas Jefferson*, I, 313-315.

2. Adams (ed.), *The Works of John Adams*, II, 513-514n.

3. Paul Leicester Ford (ed.), *The Writings of Thomas Jefferson* (New York: G. P. Putnam), X, 266-268.

4. Carl Van Doren, *Benjamin Franklin* (New York: Viking Press, 1938), pp. 550-551.

5. Ford (ed.), *The Writings of Thomas Jefferson*, X, 344-345.

6. Julian P. Boyd, *The Declaration of Independence* (Princeton University Press, 1945), pp. 19-21.

7. Frances Newton Thorpe (ed.), *Federal and State Constitutions* (Washington, 1909), I, 3ff.

8. Adams (ed.), *The Works of John Adams*, IX, 418.

9. Adams (ed.), *The Works of John Adams*, IX, 420.

10. Adams (ed.), *The Works of John Adams*, IX, 420-421.

11. Franklin B. Dexter (ed.), *The Literary Diary of Ezra Stiles* (New York, 1901), II, 23-24.

INDEX

111